CABERNET

A PHOTOGRAPHIC JOURNEY
FROM VINE TO WINE

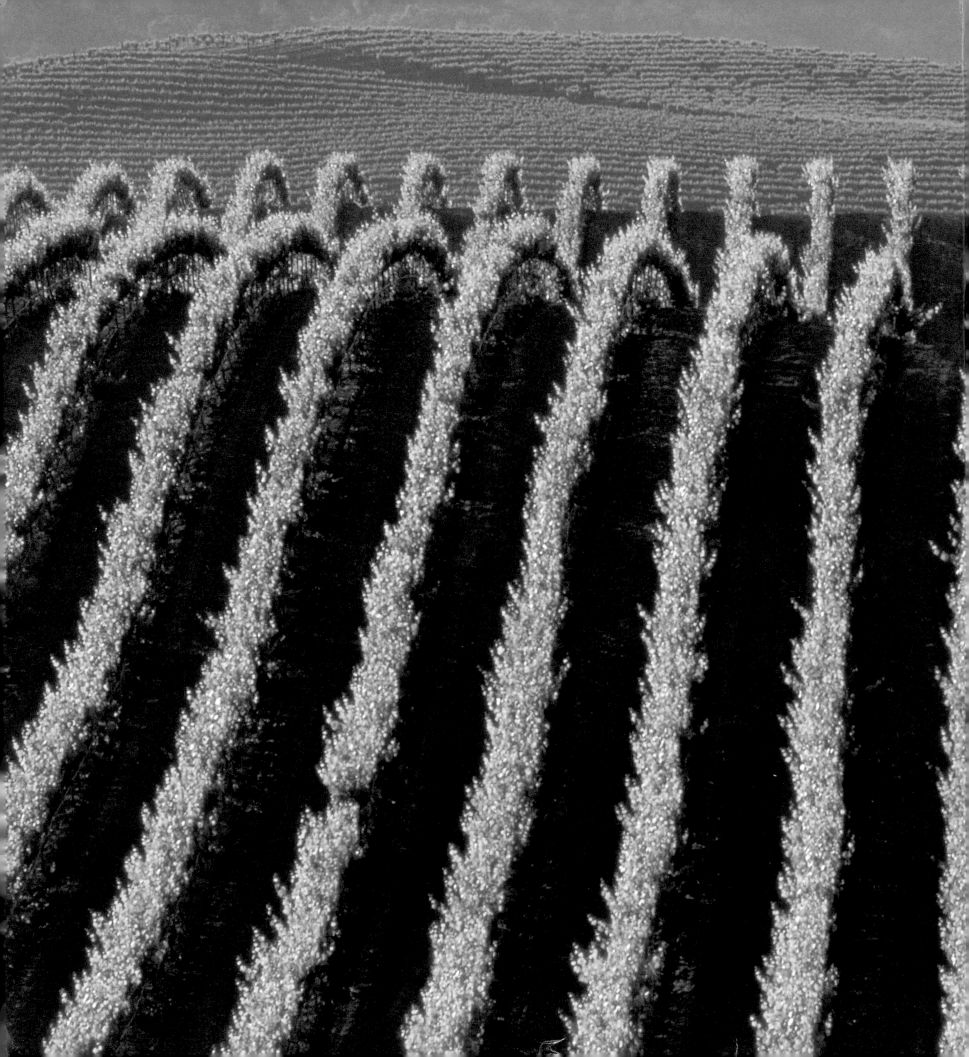

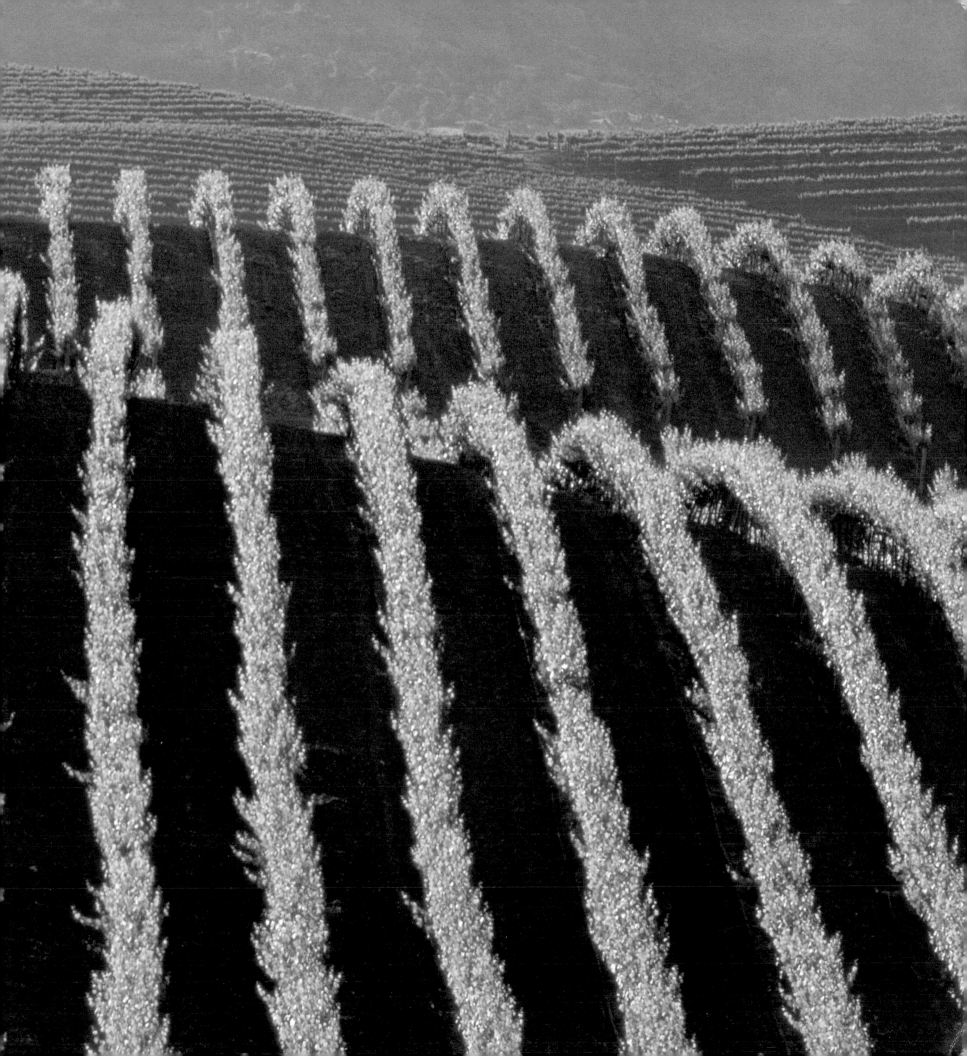

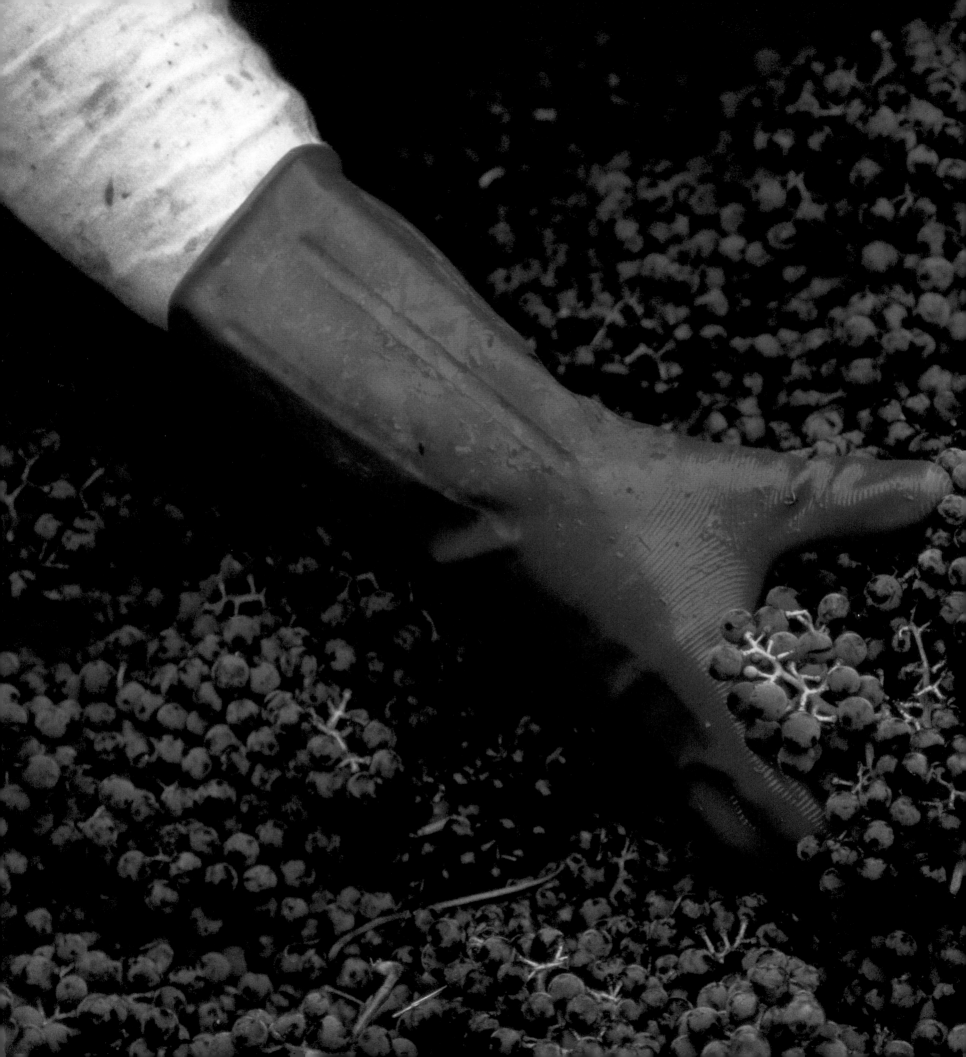

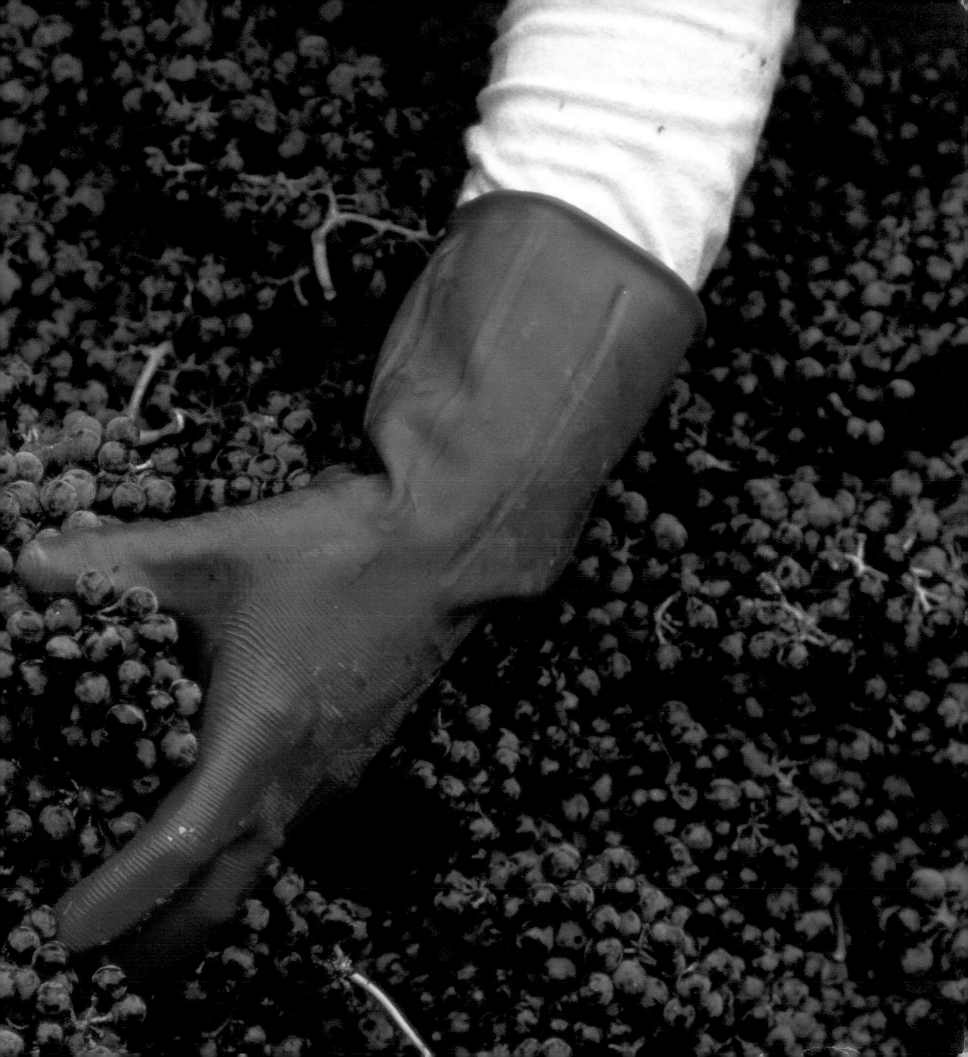

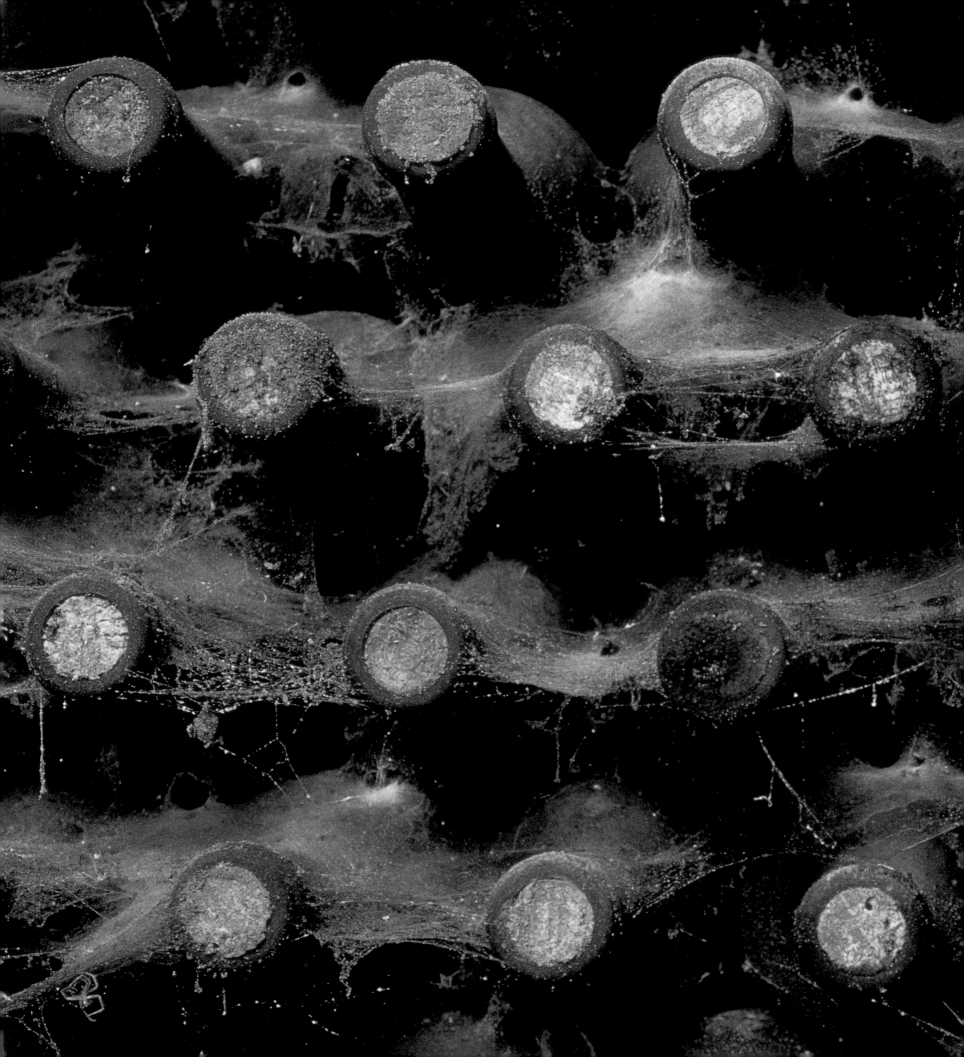

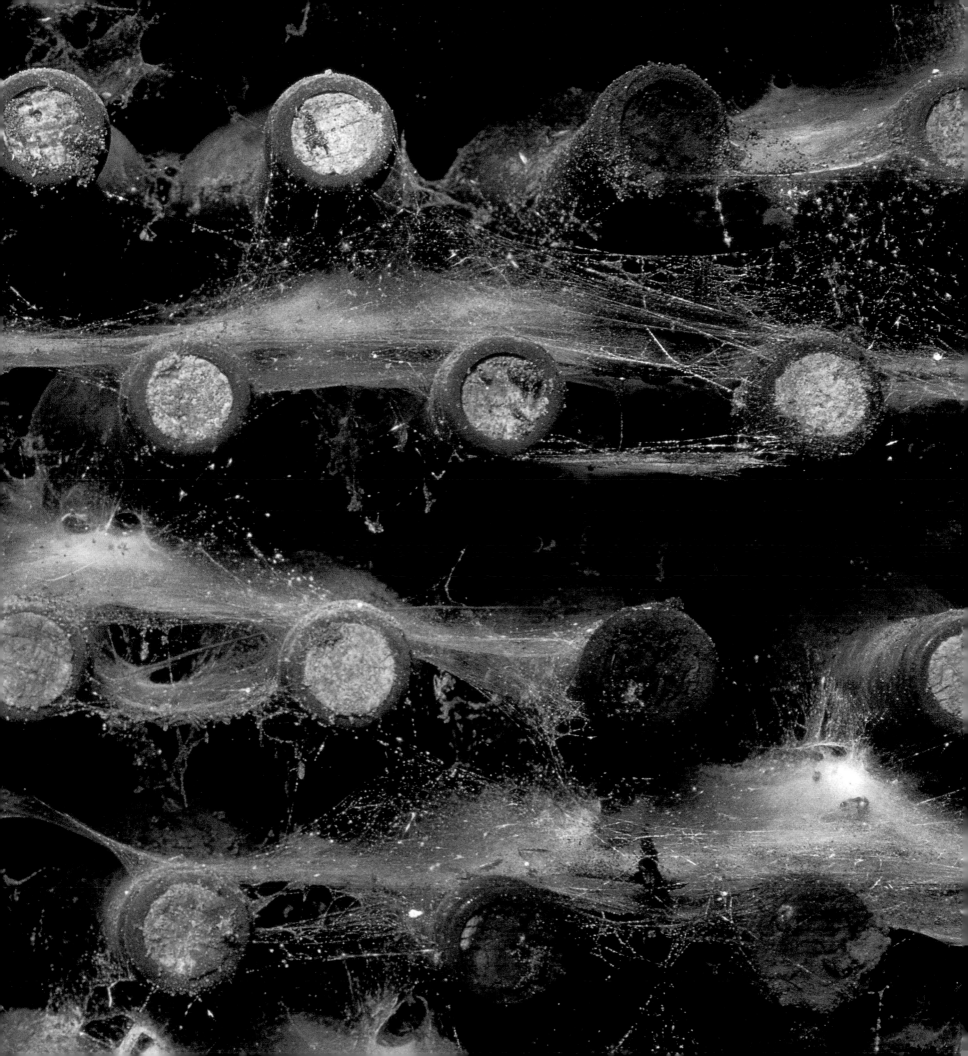

CABERNET

A PHOTOGRAPHIC JOURNEY FROM VINE TO WINE

created and photographed by

CHARLES O'REAR

text by

MICHAEL CREEDMAN

foreword by

ROBERT MONDAVI

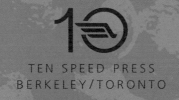

TEN SPEED PRESS
BERKELEY/TORONTO

Ten Speed Press
PO Box 7123
Berkeley, California 94707
www.tenspeed.com

Distributed in Australia by Simon and Schuster Australia, in Canada by
Ten Speed Press Canada, in New Zealand by Southern Publishers Group,
in South Africa by Real Books, in Southeast Asia by Berkeley Books, and
in the United Kingdom and Europe by Airlift Book Company.

Produced by Jennifer Barry Design, Sausalito, California
Design by Jennifer Barry and Leslie Anne Barry
Edited by Blake Hallanan
Layout Production by Kristen Wurz
Consultants: Chris Phelps, Luci Morton
Picture Editors: Laura Hunt, Jim Vestal

Charles O'Rear's photographs can be viewed at www.wineviews.com

Photographs by Charles O'Rear, copyright © 1998 by Corbis Corporation, see page 144

Jancis Robinson quote used permission of Alfred A. Knopf
from *Vines Grapes and Wines,* New York, 1986.

Library of Congress Cataloging-in-Publication Data is on file with publisher
ISBN 1-58008-373-0

First printing, 2001
Printed in Hong Kong
1 2 3 4 5 6 7 8 9 10 — 05 04 03 02 01

PRECEDING PAGES: The vines, the hands, the bottles, and the wine they make:
Cabernet Sauvignon, the incomparable aristocrat of red wines.

contents

foreword

BY ROBERT MONDAVI

I first came to Napa Valley in 1937, and a few years later my friend John Daniels, Jr. gave me an 1890 Inglenook Cabernet Sauvignon. To taste the wine, I invited John to my home along with fellow winemaking pioneer André Tchelistcheff. The wine was one of the most memorable I had ever tasted and at that moment I discovered that California could produce Cabernet on a par with the great wines of the world. That evening sparked the birth of a vision that I have carried throughout my life.

Three decades later, we built the Robert Mondavi Winery—based on the belief that we could grow exceptional grapes and make outstanding wines. The weather was favorable, the soil was right, and the people we assembled knew what they were doing. Soon we were producing a wine with its own distinct style and character.

We realized cabernet could be grown more successfully than any other red varietal and that we could achieve unsurpassed quality and consistency. Because it is picked late in the growing season, cabernet must be a strong and hearty grape that can withstand great temperature variations. This extra time on the vine brings the depth and complexity of flavor that helps make Cabernet so great. That's why I like to call it the king of red wine, and the noblest of them all.

Since those early days in Napa Valley, I have visited hundreds of wineries all over the world. In my travels I've been impressed by the variety of ways in which grapes are grown and wine is made. I return home again and again wishing to share all I have learned about the production of exceptional wines.

A wish to share my knowledge on the art of winemaking contributed to the creation of this book. Recently, Charles O'Rear asked for my recommendations of the most important wine-producing regions in the world. It was that conversation that led him to travel for more than a year, following the wine harvests around the globe. To make many of the photographs for this book, he went to Europe, South America, South Africa, Australia, and New Zealand, as well as to our own vineyards here in America.

I don't know of any other photographer who has taken his love and knowledge of wine and has been able to give us such a complete visual presentation as is in this outstanding book. With his camera, Charles goes behind the scenes, unveiling much of the mystery and soul which brings a unique and distinctive character to a great glass of Cabernet. It is with much pride that I welcome you to this first serious photography book devoted solely to Cabernet.

"Cabernet is king because it can be grown more successfully than any other

ROBERT MONDAVI
CHAIRMAN OF THE BOARD, ROBERT MONDAVI WINERY

red varietal and achieves an unsurpassed quality and consistency worldwide."

introduction

BY CHARLES O'REAR

There's something magical about a great Cabernet Sauvignon. It's something that goes beyond the taste and the smell and the way it feels on the palate. It's not something you can precisely describe, but you can see it in the hands and eyes of those who tend the vines and crush the grapes. You can glimpse it in the smiles of those who drink and prize the wine. And you can sense it in the way cabernet vineyards and wineries all over the world are so carefully tended and maintained.

I have been fascinated with wine for most of my life and have studied it enough to understand the process from planting the vines to aging the wine. Yet, I still marvel at the mysterious process that somehow transforms a cluster of grapes into a divine nectar, especially into Cabernet Sauvignon, the king of wines.

Photographing for *National Geographic* magazine for twenty-five years (and more recently for Bill Gates' archive, Corbis Corporation) I've had the opportunity to travel the world making pictures of everything from technology to archeology. Everywhere I've traveled within the temperate latitudes of the world, I've noticed that winemaking is an important part of life. And everywhere that people are involved in the business of making wine, there's a *joie de vivre* that surpasses anything I've experienced. I think it's because almost everyone concerned with

making wine, from the château owner to those who tend the grapes and rack the barrels, seems to love what he or she does.

To create photographs for this book, I traveled for more than a year visiting the major wine-producing regions in the world. Some of those places, such as South Africa, New Zealand, and Chile, may not spring instantly to mind as wine production centers. But they do grow grapes in those nations and make some excellent wines, too, including Cabernet Sauvignon.

By visiting the world's chief grape-growing countries and photographing their wineries, I've had the opportunity to capture the fascinating visual journey from vine to wine.

At home in California's Napa Valley, I've been privileged to become friends with serious winemakers, including the owners of some of the greatest wineries on earth. These opportunities have placed me in a unique position to document the process and the lifestyle that surrounds this ancient art.

This book is not just about wine, though. It's about a very specific wine: Cabernet Sauvignon, perhaps the most aristocratic

The sun never sets on and winter never comes to the world of wine. Every season of the year, wine grapes are in harvest somewhere on Earth throughout two bands located between 30 degrees and 50 degrees north and south of the equator *(right)*.

of the half dozen major grape varietals in world commerce. Wine experts agree that more fine wine is made with cabernet than any other grape. It's also the most popular wine in the world.

Cabernet's popularity didn't develop overnight. Some experts think the cabernet vine dates back to biblical times in the Adriatic region of Italy or Greece. Others suggest that the vines were imported by Romans from Russia to France nearly 2,000 years ago, but under a different name. Even the origin of the word Cabernet is very much in doubt. But it's believed that Sauvignon comes from the French word *sauvage*, or wild.

Documented records of Cabernet Sauvignon go back only about two centuries ago to the Bordeaux region of France. By that time, anyone with a nose for wine and a purse fat enough to pay the price recognized the high quality of wine made from Cabernet Sauvignon, or *Vidure*, as the grape was sometimes called.

Early travelers began carrying cuttings from those vines all over the world. A Hungarian count probably brought them to Northern California, the Spanish took them to Chile, and the Huguenots carried cabernet cuttings to South Africa. From

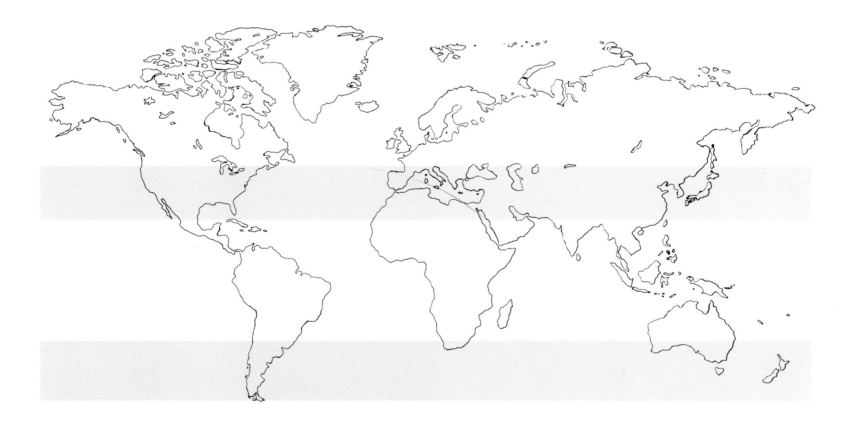

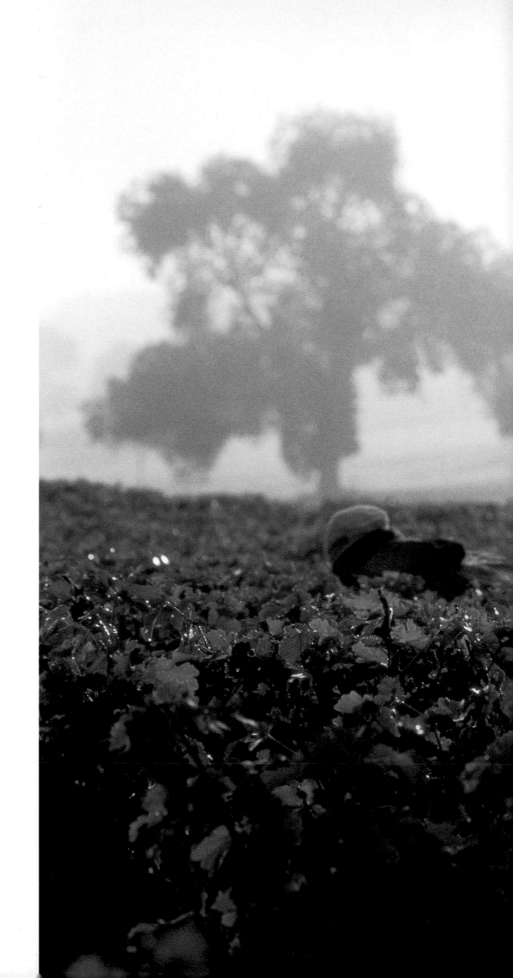

South Africa, they were carried on to Australia.

One reason cabernet took root in all those places is because it is a hardy grape. It can grow and survive in many climates. It thrives in meager, rocky soil. It stubbornly survives drought and flood. And its thick, waxy skin is resistant to rot.

Cabernet is more expensive to produce than most other wines for three reasons: First, the vineyards yield less fruit per vine than other varietals. It also requires more blending because it achieves its lofty status mainly when other wines such as Cabernet Franc are added in small proportions. Finally, with its rich complexity of flavors, Cabernet needs more time in storage.

So, here in your hands are the photographs that provide a behind-the-scenes look at what it takes to produce the finest of the world's wines. The following pages don't just illustrate the process of growing and making Cabernet. They also reflect the spirit of the people who keep the art of winemaking alive.

My hope is that you'll enjoy the book in the same way you enjoy the wine and that it will leave a pleasant memory that brings you back, again and again.

In the cool of early morning, *vendangeurs* in the Médoc region of France gently pour just-picked grapes into a specially designed backpack. The careful treatment keeps the grapes whole until the moment they are crushed at the winery.

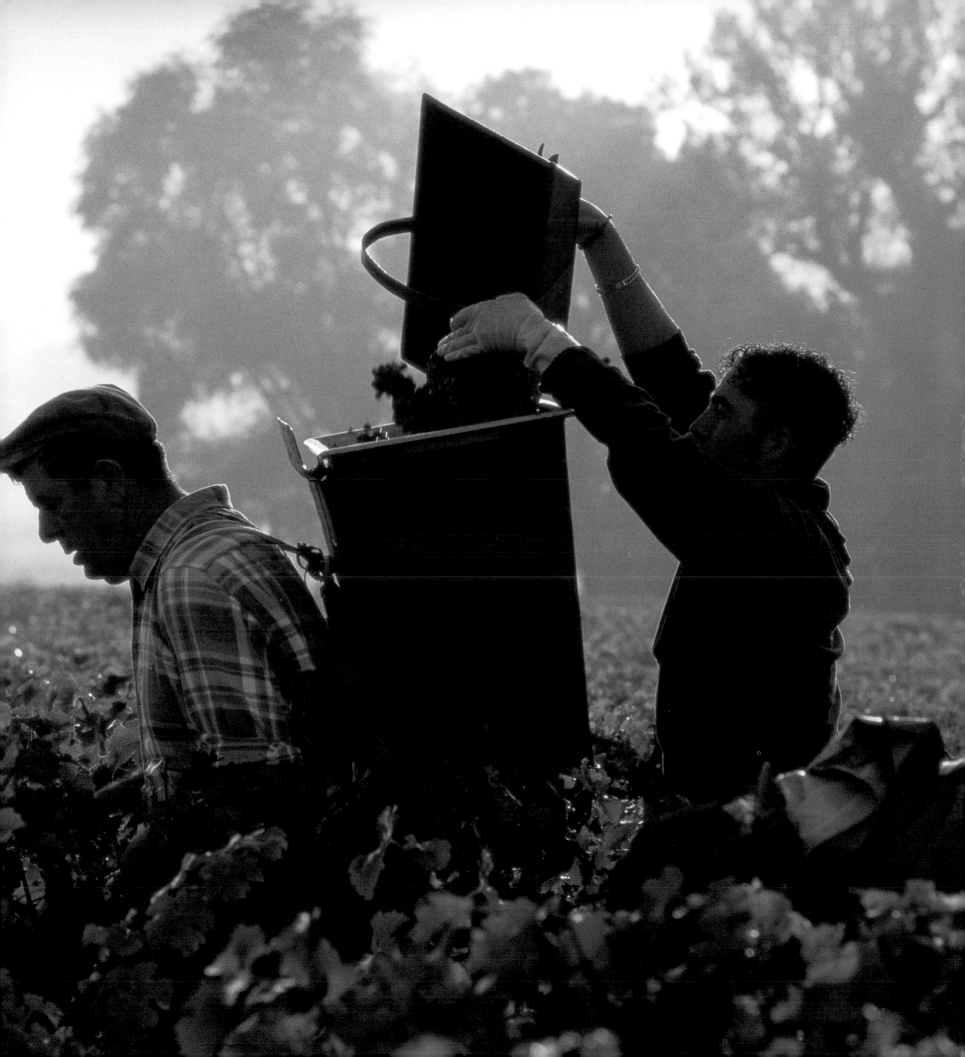

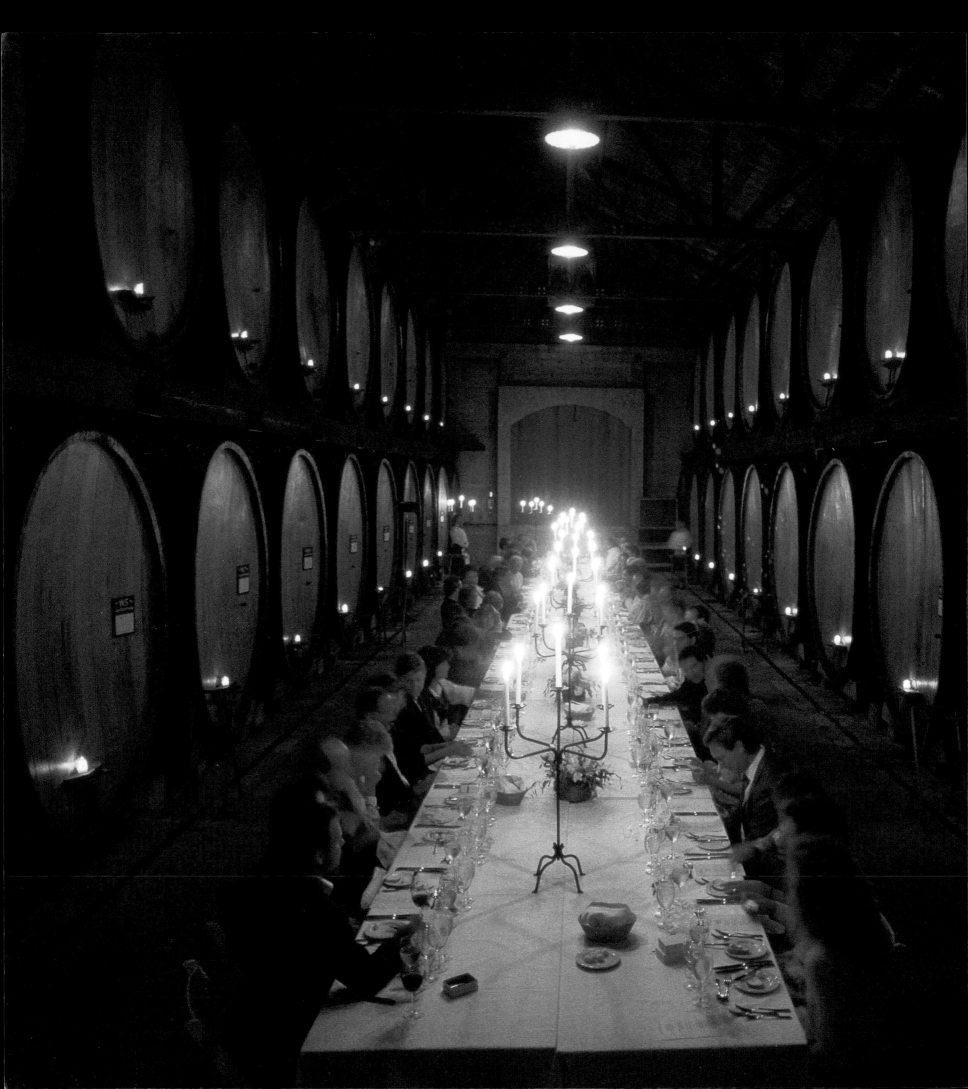

chapter one

CABERNET

the aristocrat

CABERNET: THE ARISTOCRAT

In all of history, in all of fiction, in all of our lives, wine in some way plays a part.

Jesus shared wine with his disciples.

The Romans drank toasts to their "invincible" empire.

It was also the wine that helped Robin Hood and his men make merry.

And whenever lovers dine, friends come together, or families reunite, wine is what turns the meeting into an occasion.

Throughout the world, there is no wine more respected, better known, and more popular than Cabernet Sauvignon. That popularity is based on more than its distinctive flavor or the toughness of the vines that produce the grapes. There's something entirely regal about the deep purple of Cabernet as it pours from the bottle—as it shimmers in a glass. Even more, there's something powerful about its mystique . . . a combination of taste and history that's impossible to define.

What's easy to explain is why it is the aristocratic: because it is the standard against which other wines are judged.

Cabernet Sauvignon isn't a wine for beginners. Its flavor is usually too strong for those unaccustomed to wine. No matter where it is grown, it has a distinct flavor and an identifiable aroma. In a way, Cabernet is like a brash kid from the big city. It's assertive and tough and doesn't make itself easily accessible. But become its friend, understand its character, appreciate its complexities, and Cabernet Sauvignon becomes a hero. It

provides a window, if only in hints and tastes, of sun-splashed vineyards, chateaux in Europe, cool caves filled with wood barrels, and satisfied workers toiling in the terraces.

If fine wine appeals to all our senses, then it's Cabernet that captures them all.

For example, you can almost listen to the silence in a glass of Cabernet and hear the echoes of long gone laughter, the whisper of indiscrete proposals, the clink of glasses, or the pounding of a romantic surf.

If you look into the deep, dark elixir you may glimpse a shadow of candlelight, a twinkle of stars, a blaze of gemstones, or the searchlights of an opening night.

Recognize in the aromas of Cabernet the moist earth in the morning as it starts to absorb the sun's rays, the fruit of the grape and the hints that could include black pepper, clove, or vanilla.

Taste a complex combination of flavors that have often been described as blackcurrant, chocolate, or berries.

And with each sip feel a kind of liquid velvet on the palate. Test the sensation on the tongue that is produced by Cabernet Sauvignon. Some say it feels like burnished copper while others claim Cabernet lands in the mouth like a daring flock of pheasants all arriving at the same time. For wine is not just a drink. It's an entry point to a richer world of friendship, parties, meditation, and romance. And there's no wine that makes a more elegant entrance than Cabernet Sauvignon.

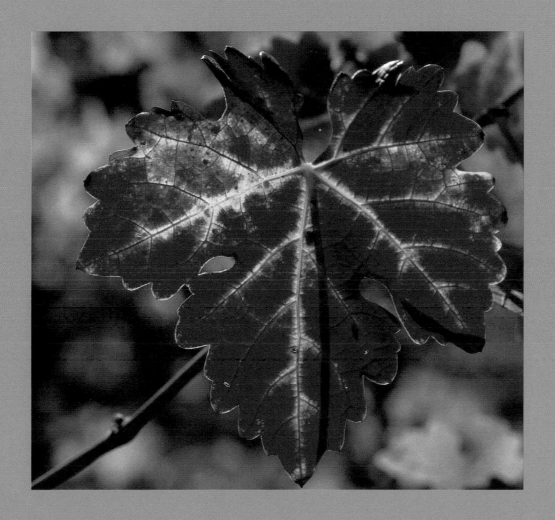

Wine, candles, and pageantry delight sixty guests at a dinner in
the Cask Room at Merryvale Vineyards in St. Helena, California *(preceding page)*.
A cabernet leaf turns a rich red when the vines go dormant in autumn *(above)*.

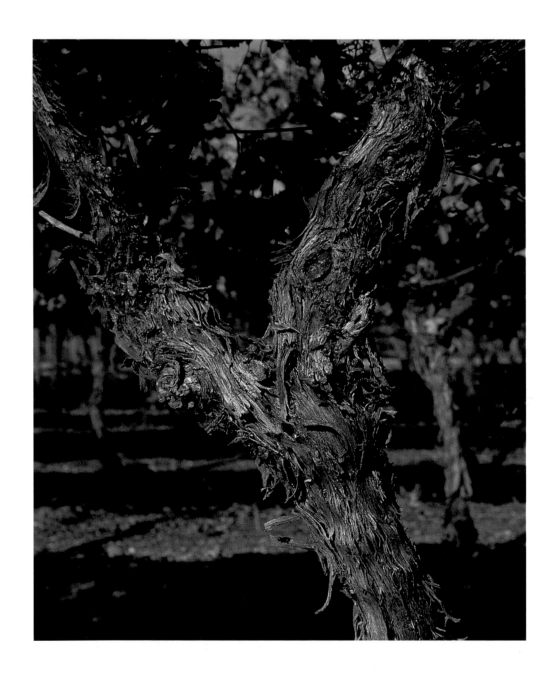

The legendary toughness of the cabernet vine is expressed in this twisted trunk in
the Coonawarra region of Australia, the country's most popular cabernet-growing area *(above)*.
The widely spaced rows at this California vineyard *(right)* were originally laid out to accommodate
horse-drawn wagons. Today, more densely planted vineyards can produce much more wine
per acre, but a few skeptics contend the quality has slipped slightly.

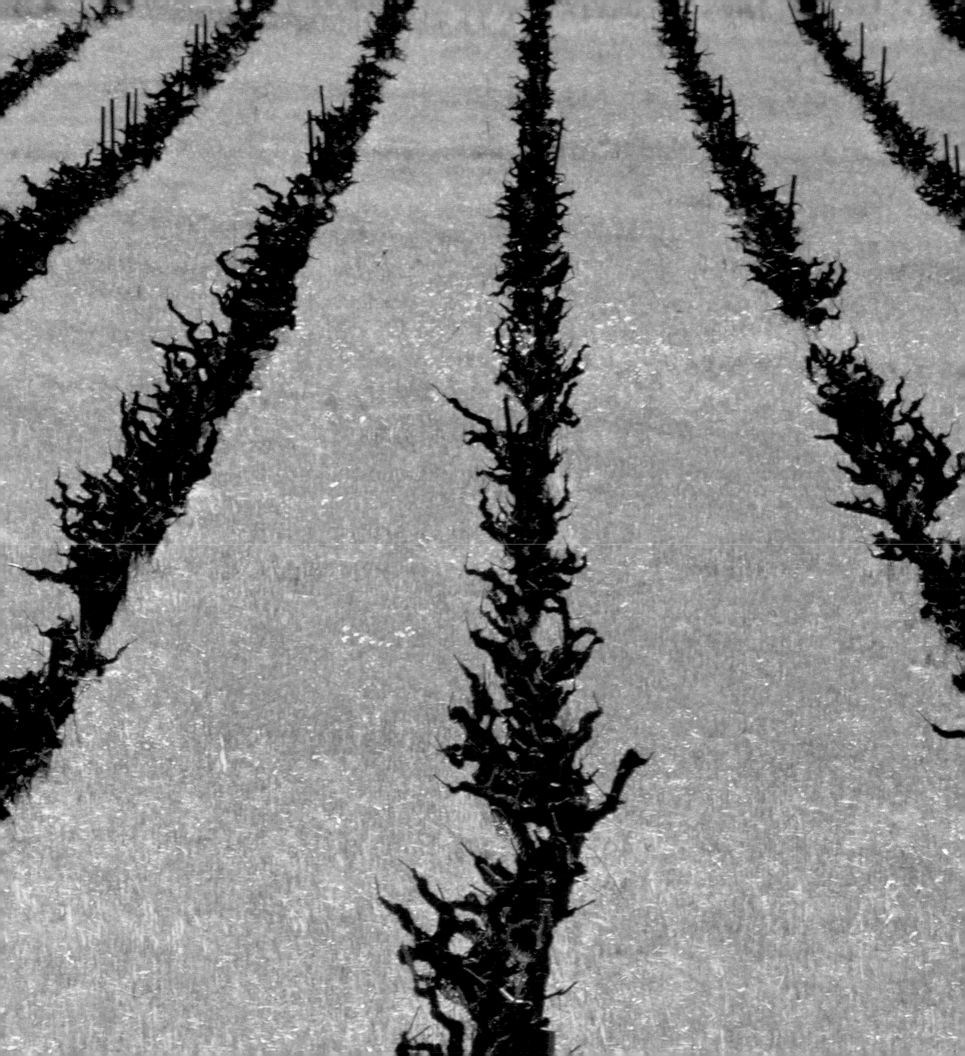

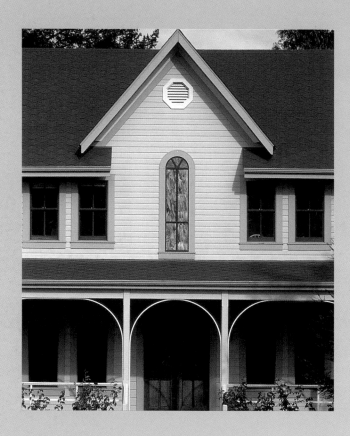

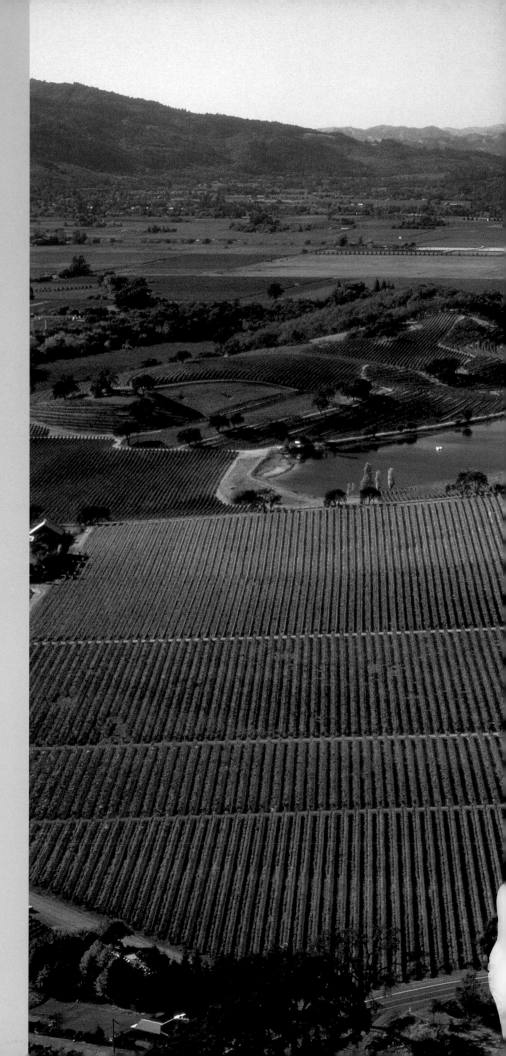

Among the unique buildings in the Napa Valley is
Beckstoffer Vineyard farm center, which was designed to
reflect early California architecture *(above)*. Mount St. Helena,
at 4,343 feet, stands guard in the distance above the famed
Napa Valley 40 miles northeast of San Francisco.
In the foreground, a dry riverbed winds slowly past several
hundred vineyards soaking up the sunshine *(right)*.

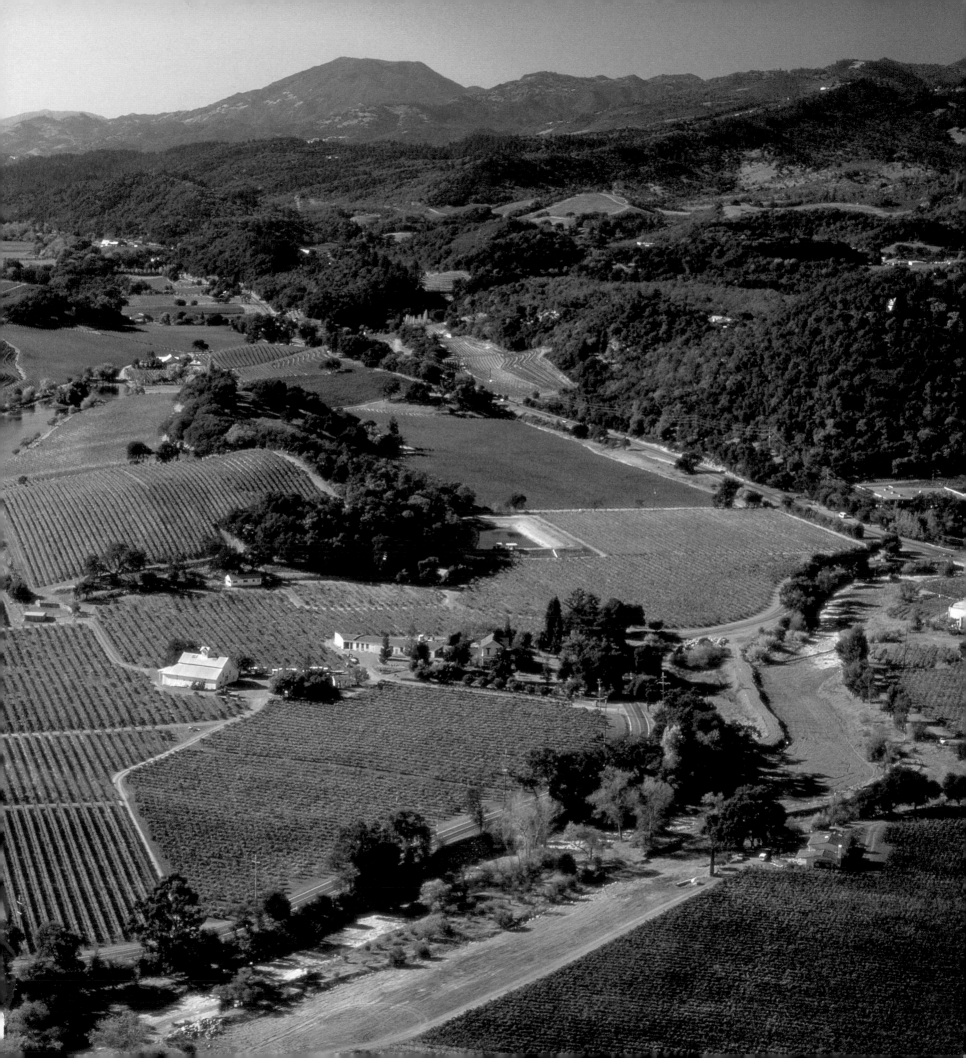

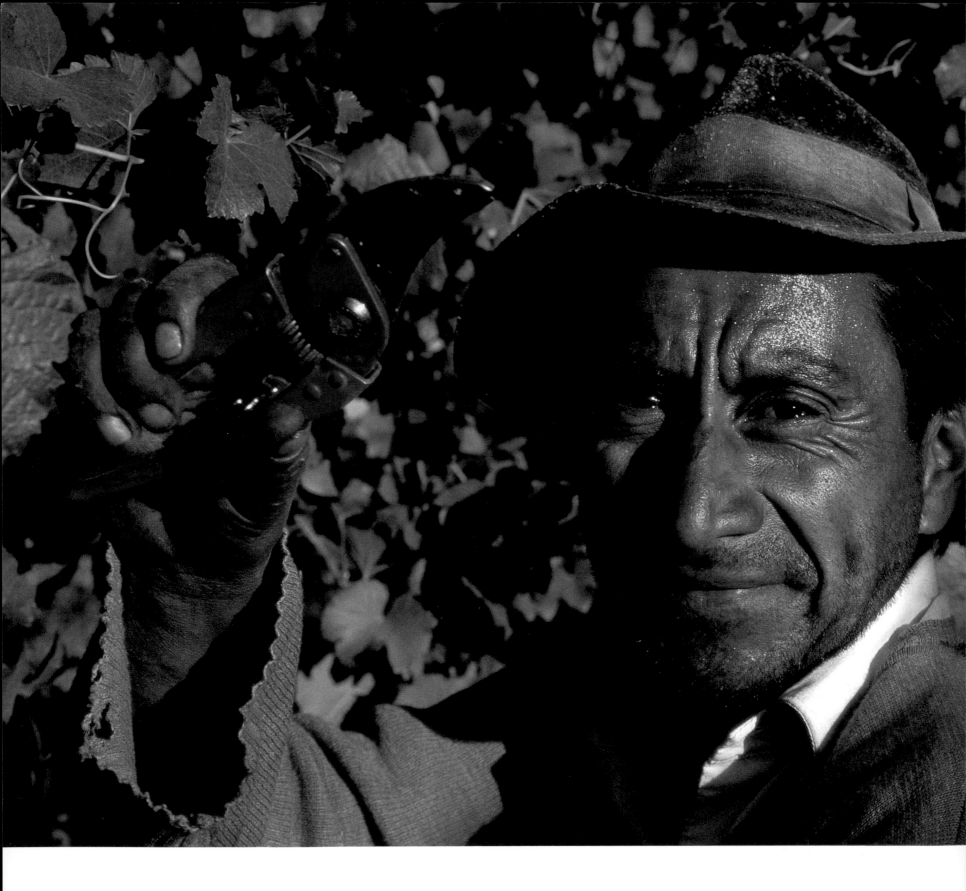

A grape picker from Chile shows his shears to a visitor *(above)*. Cabernet grapes on the vine at Grace Family Vineyard in St. Helena, the geographical center of Napa Valley, just minutes before they were picked *(top right)*. Signpost on New Zealand's South Island reflects the growing interest in Cabernet Sauvignon *(right)*.

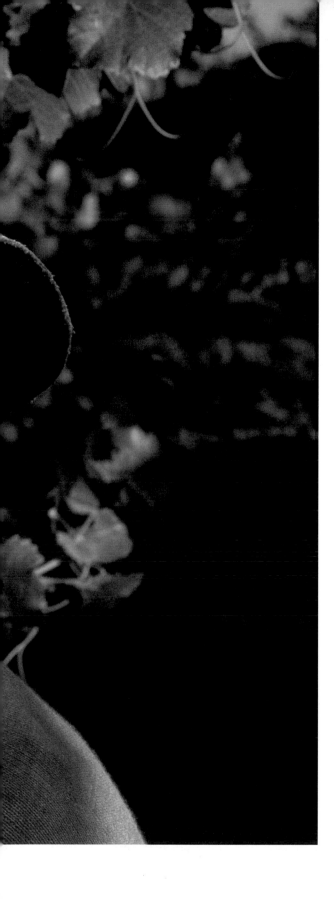
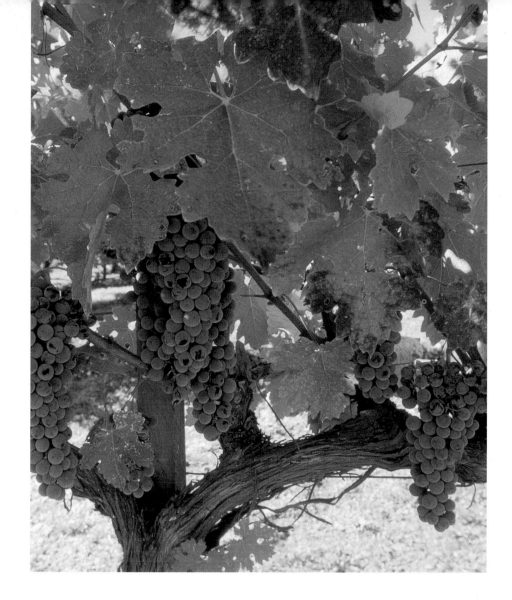
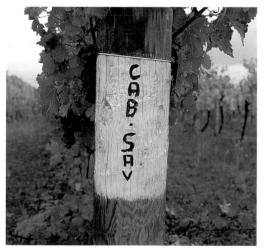

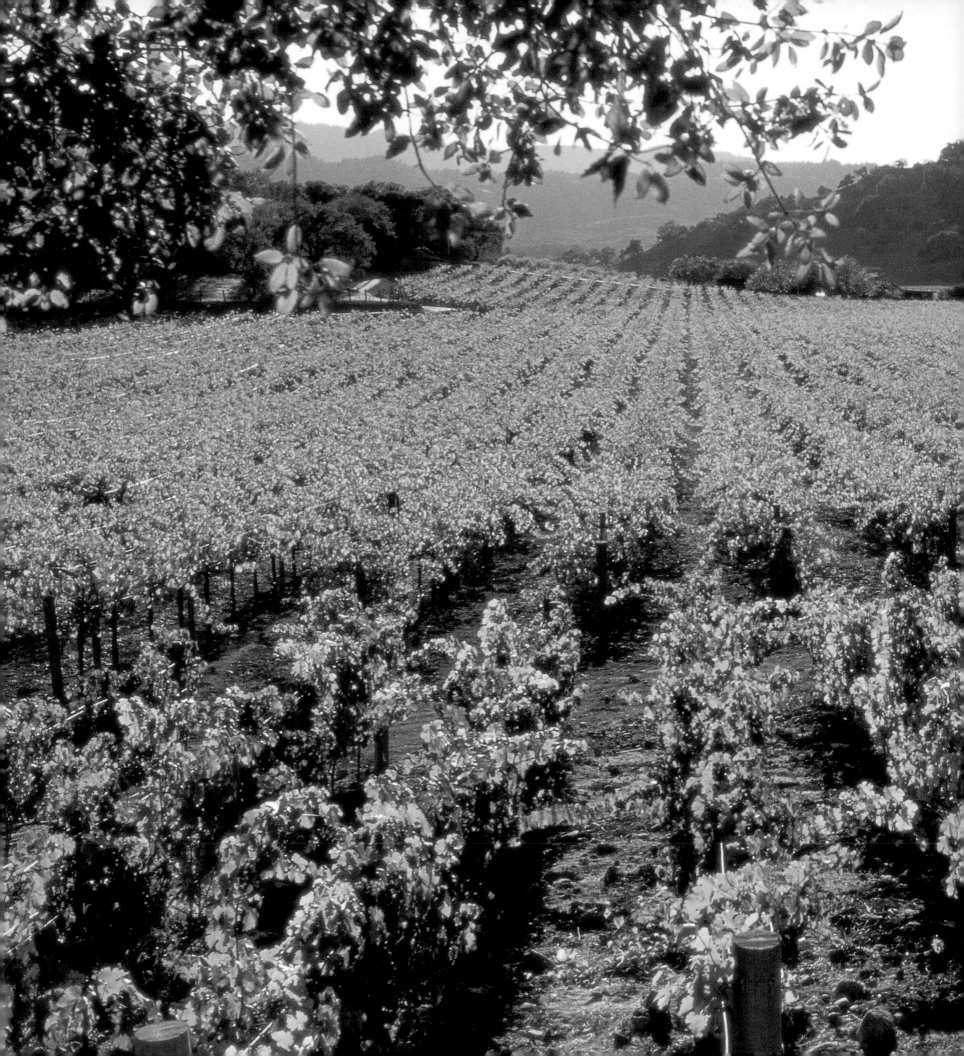

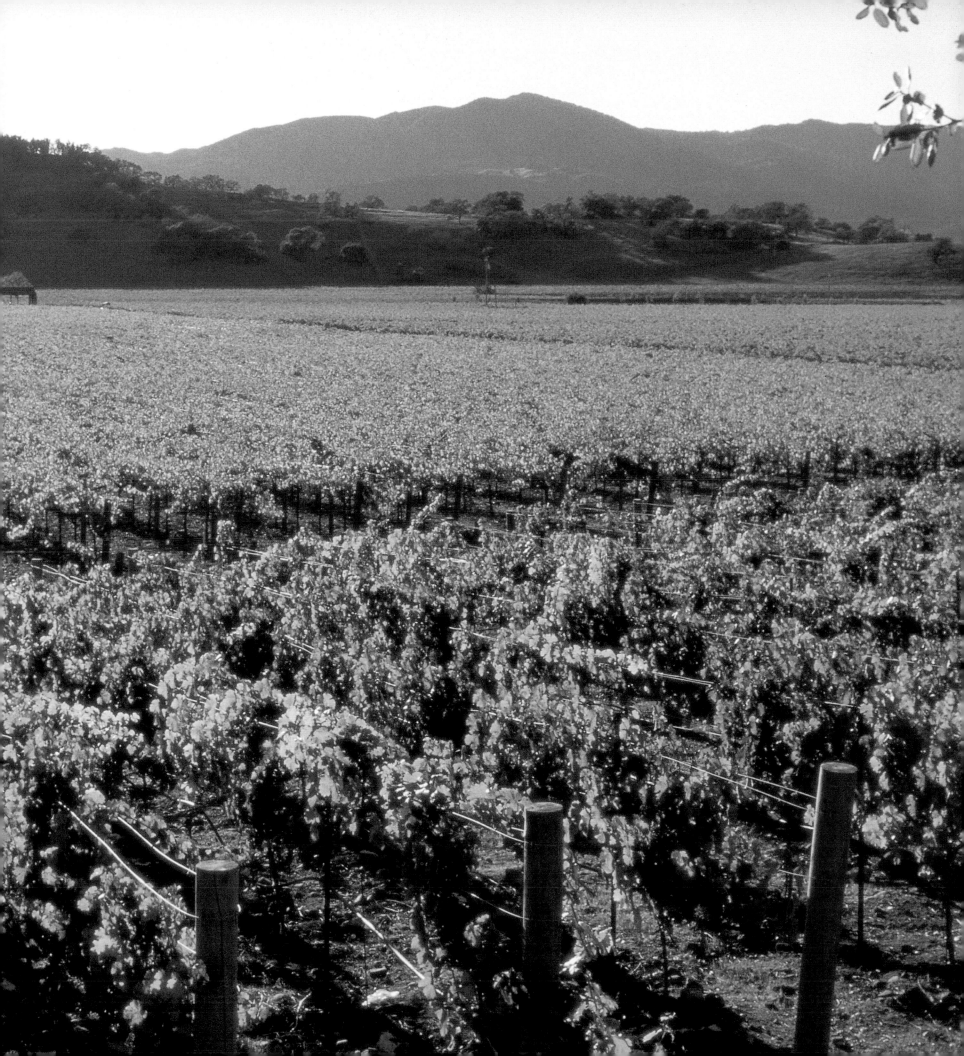

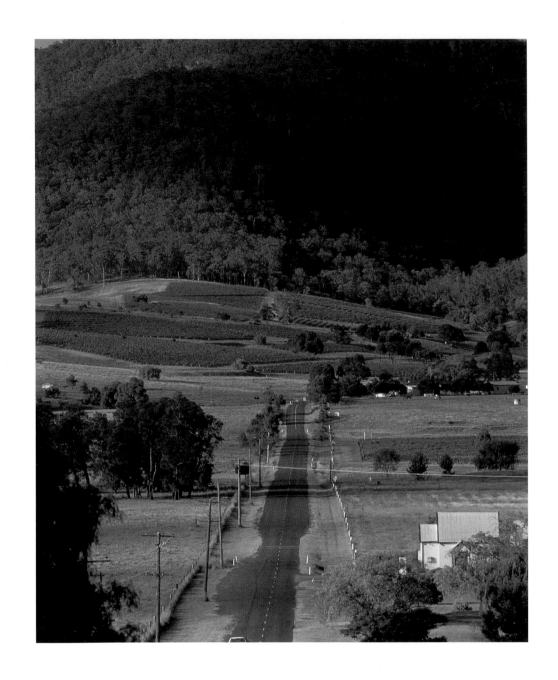

Do vineyards grow in the world's most beautiful places, or do vineyards make
ordinary places beautiful? No matter what the answer, these locations unquestionably qualify
as beautiful: the Napa Valley *(preceding pages)*, Hunter Valley of Australia *(above)*,
and the vineyards of Château Latour, near Bordeaux *(right)*.

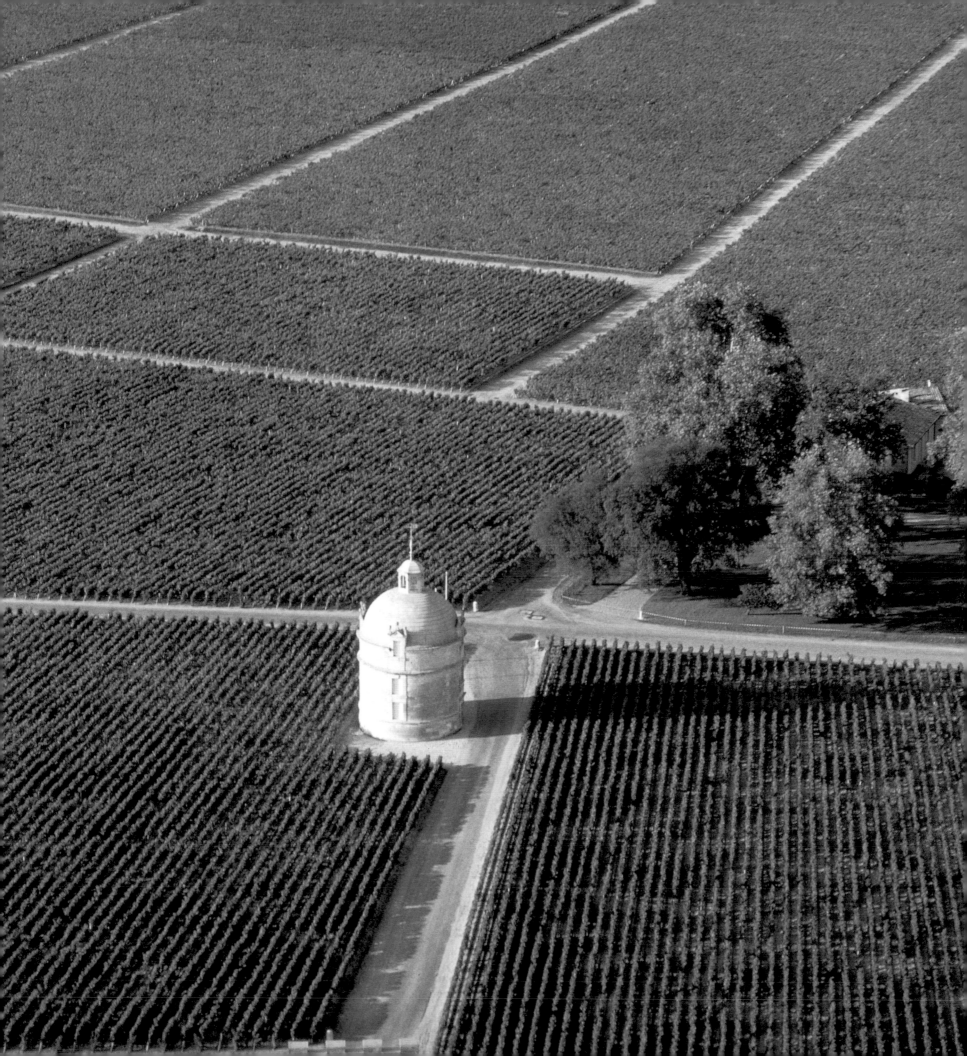

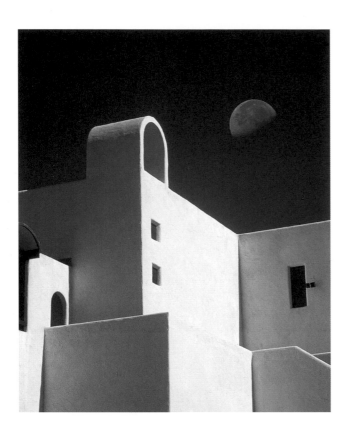

When winery owners went to Europe for cabernet vine cuttings, they were often influenced by the architecture— for example, the Greek monastery-style winery of Sterling Vineyards in the Napa Valley *(above)* and the Cape Dutch-style facade at Morgenhof Winery, near Cape Town, South Africa *(right)*.

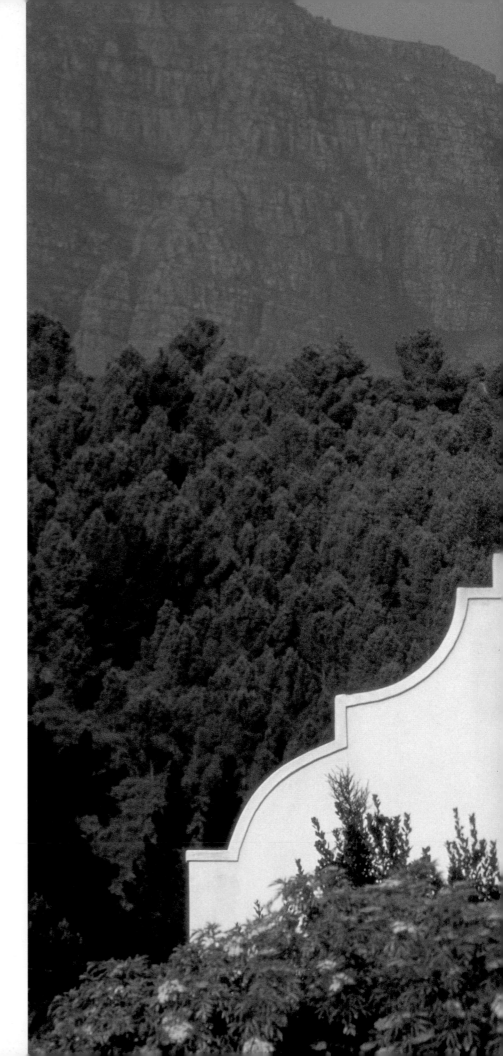

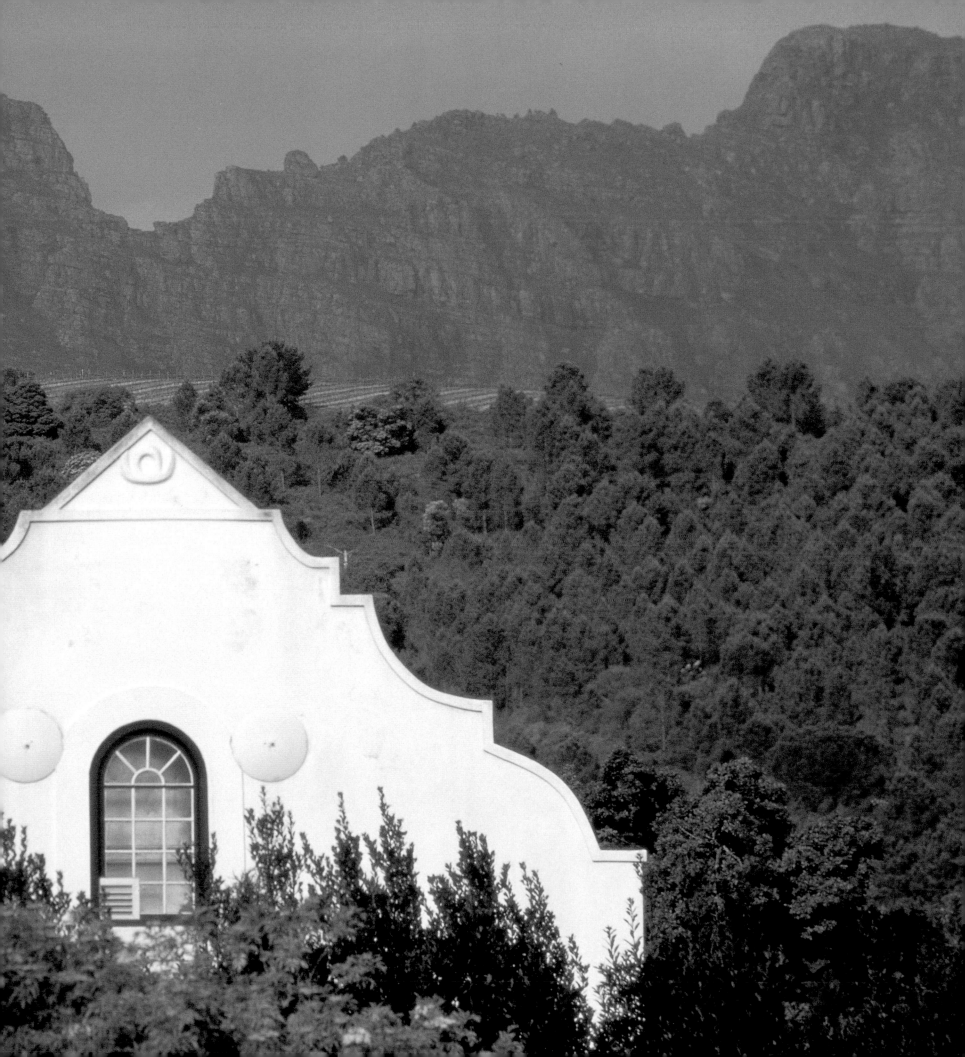

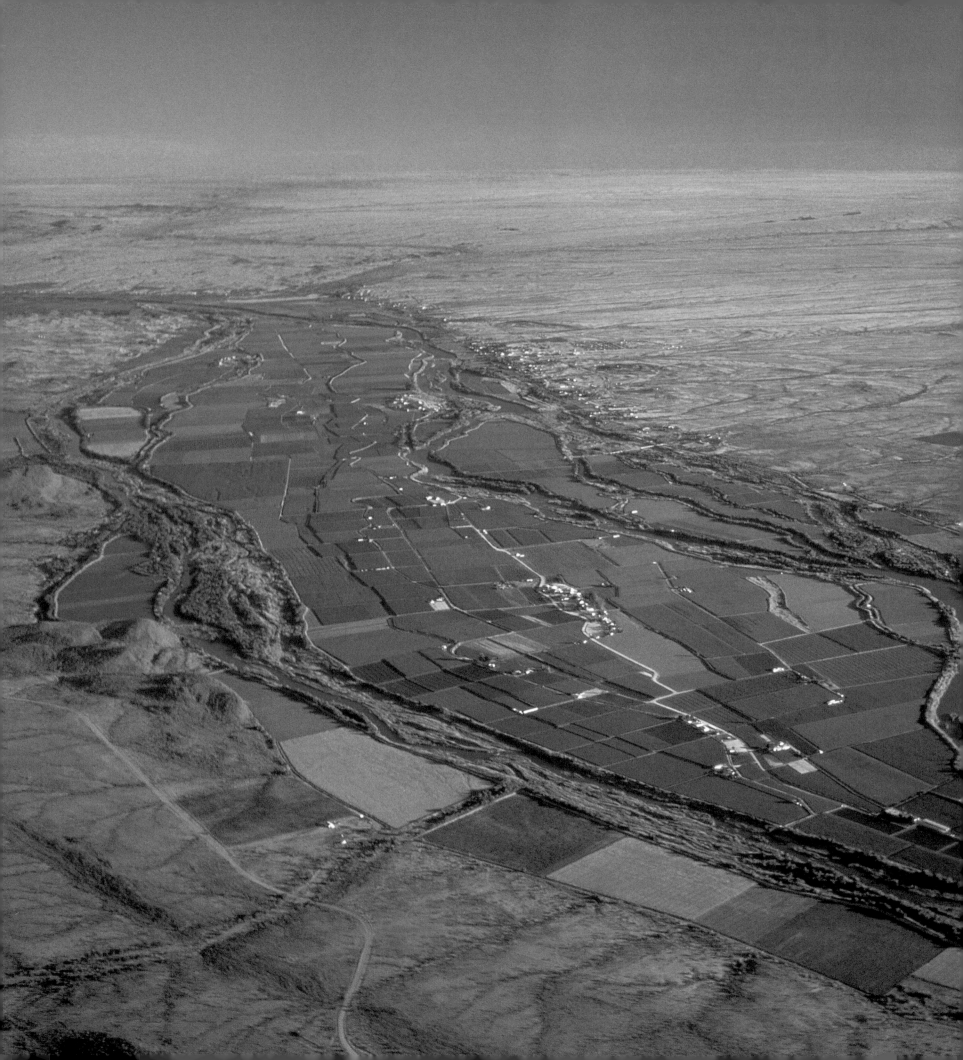

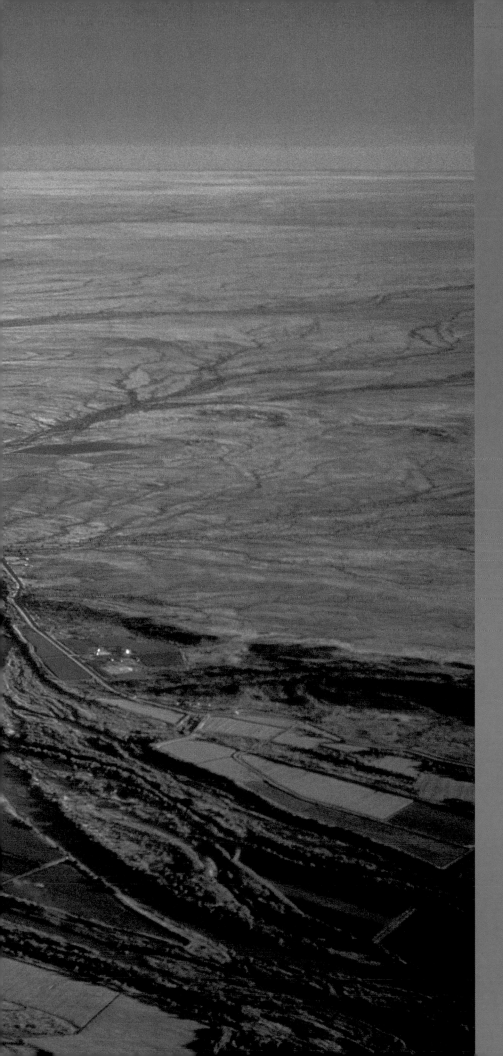

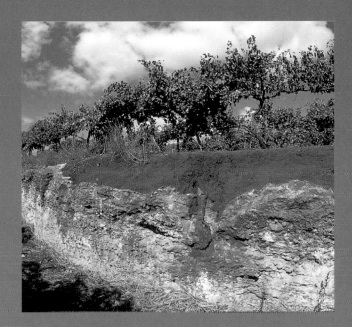

A virtual oasis in the South African desert,
the Orange River Valley *(left)* grows a heat-tolerant varietal
known as ruby cabernet. In the Coonawarra region
of Australia, a demonstration vineyard shows the famous
"terra rossa" red soil and the distinctive extended
root system of cabernet *(above)*.

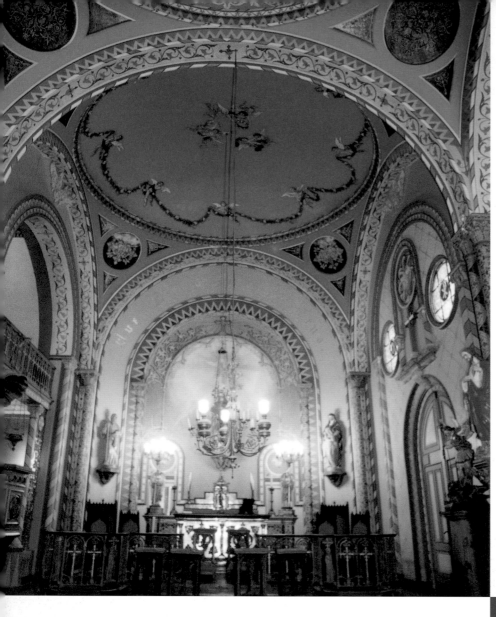

Making wine has historically been linked with social and economic power. Missionaries typically planted grapes wherever they established their religion in order to make sacramental wine. Chapels in wineries that produce Cabernet such as Viña Santa Rita in Chile *(above)* and Vega Sicilia in central Spain *(right)* reflect that tradition. Often, the masters of large estates planted vineyards to make wine for themselves and sold the surplus in the local markets. The English gardens of Newton Vineyards in the Napa Valley *(top right)* and Château Marbuzet in the Médoc region are reminiscent of the feudal manors *(far right)*.

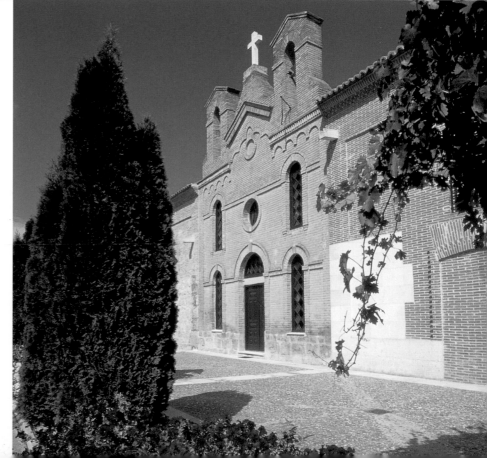

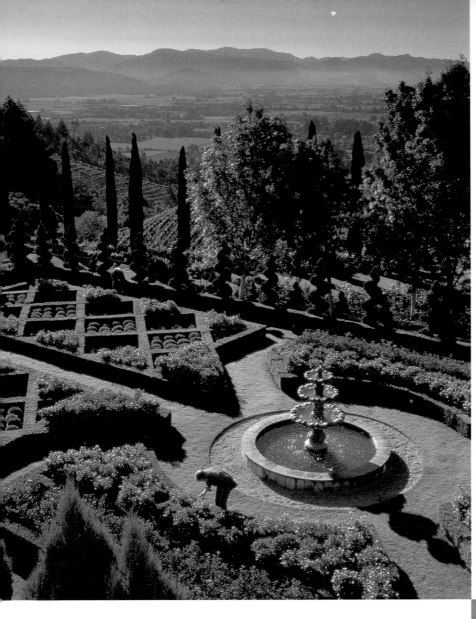

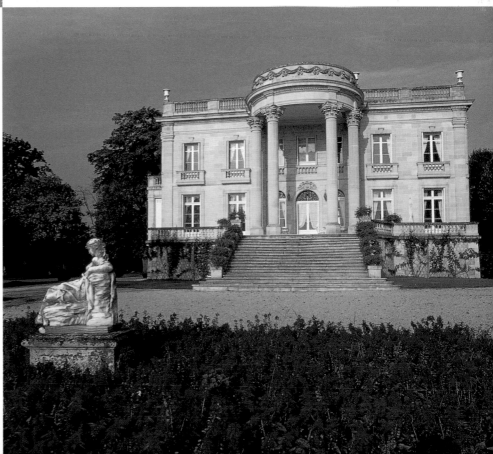

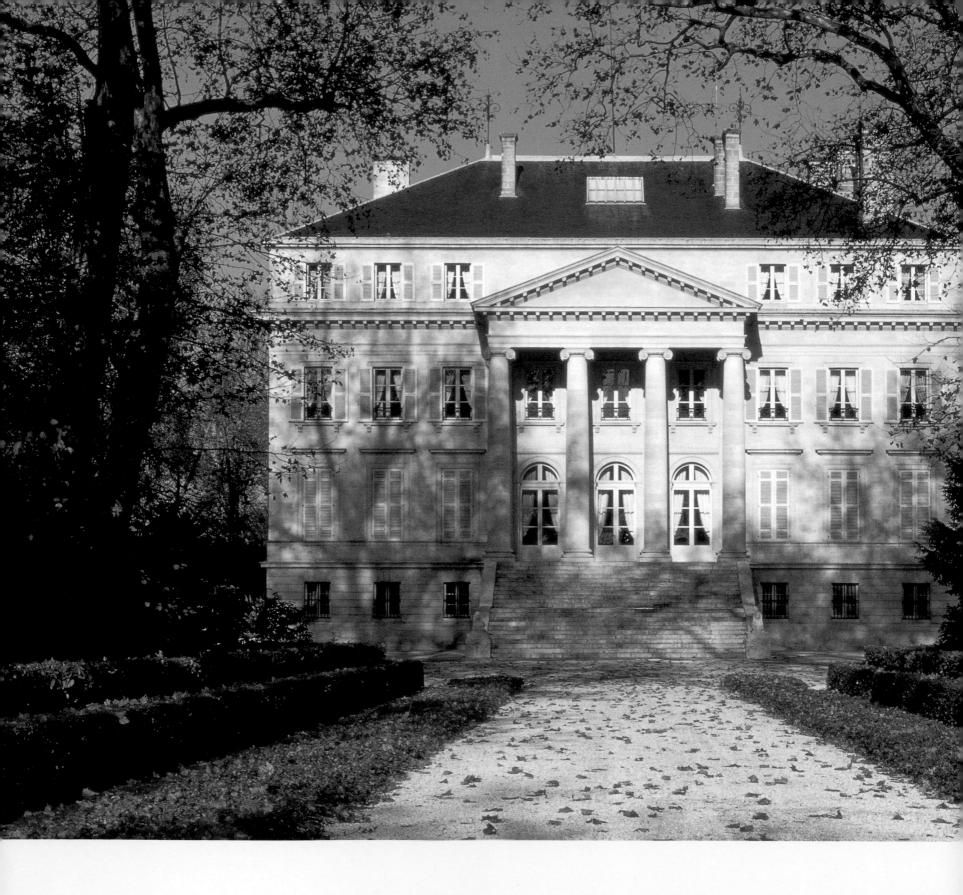

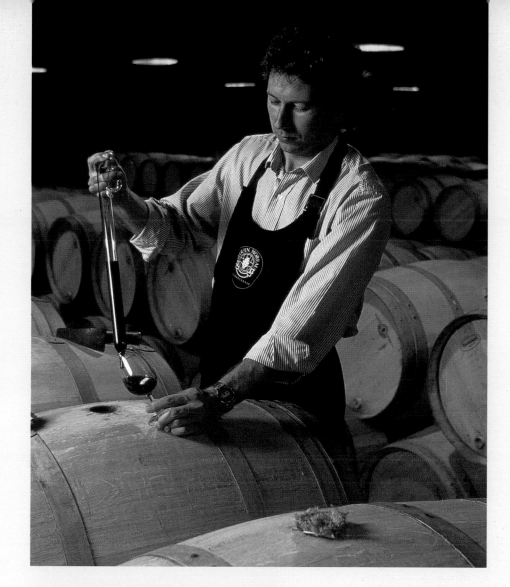

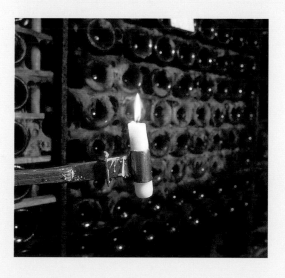

france

If there were a capitol building for the world's cabernet growers, Château Margaux in Bordeaux might be it *(left)*.

French vintners in the Médoc region established the Cabernet Sauvignon style and their wine today remains the standard against which other wines are judged. The maître de chais of Cos d'Estournel in Bordeaux samples last year's vintage *(top)*.

A candle spreads light deep in the aging cave of Château Mouton-Rothschild *(above)*.

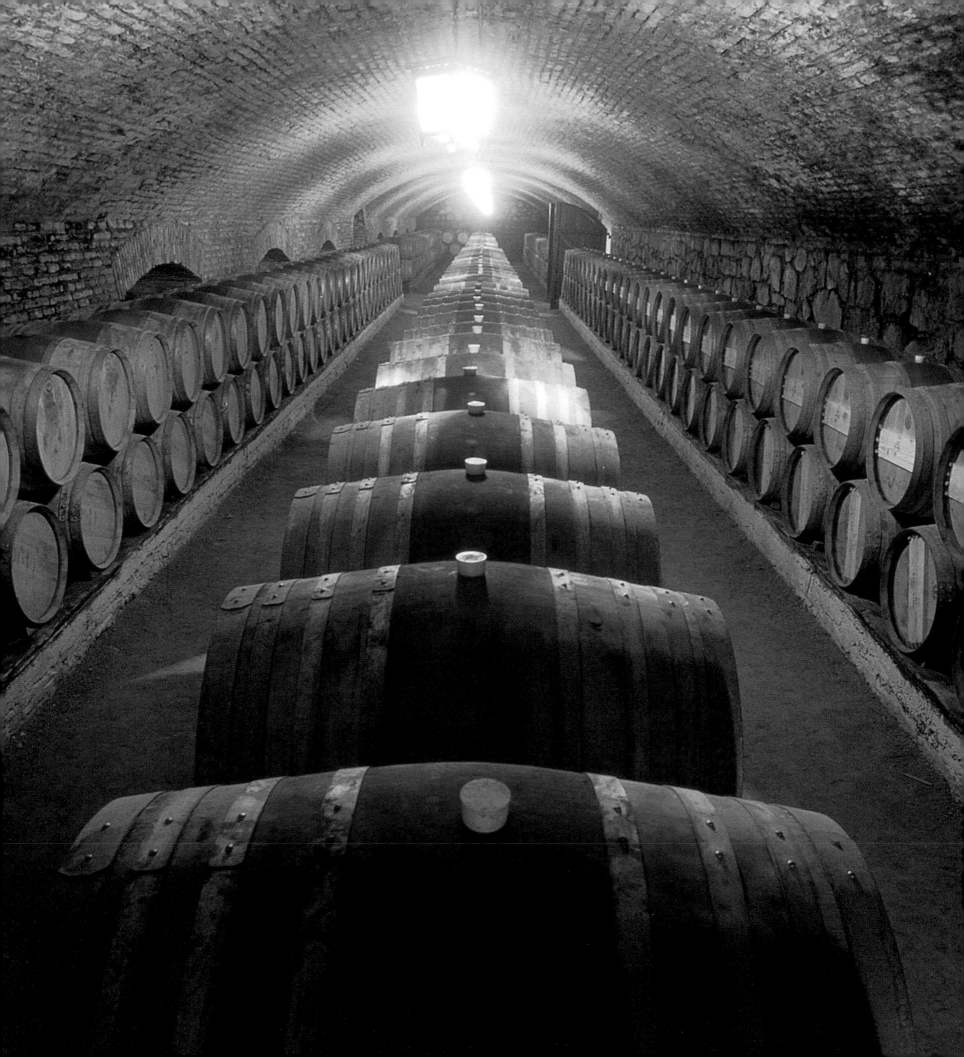

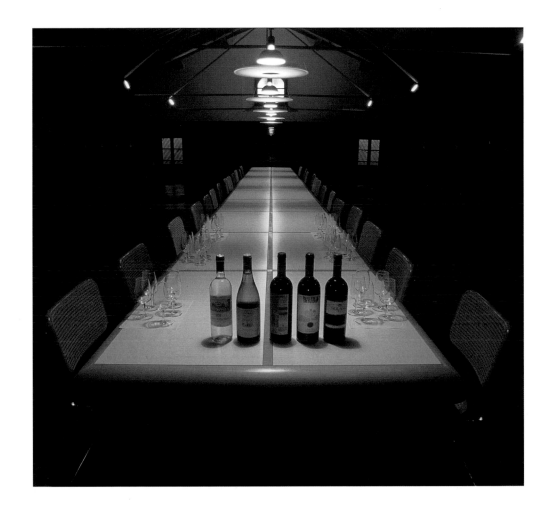

A transformation is quietly taking place in the underground cellars of
Errazuriz Estates near Santiago, Chile *(left)*. Aging in oak barrels produces a metamorphosis
in Cabernet Sauvignon wine. It becomes softer and more accessible. Tasting rooms like
this one at Antinori near Florence, Italy *(above)*, are an important showcase where wineries
present their product to wholesalers, distributors, and special visitors.

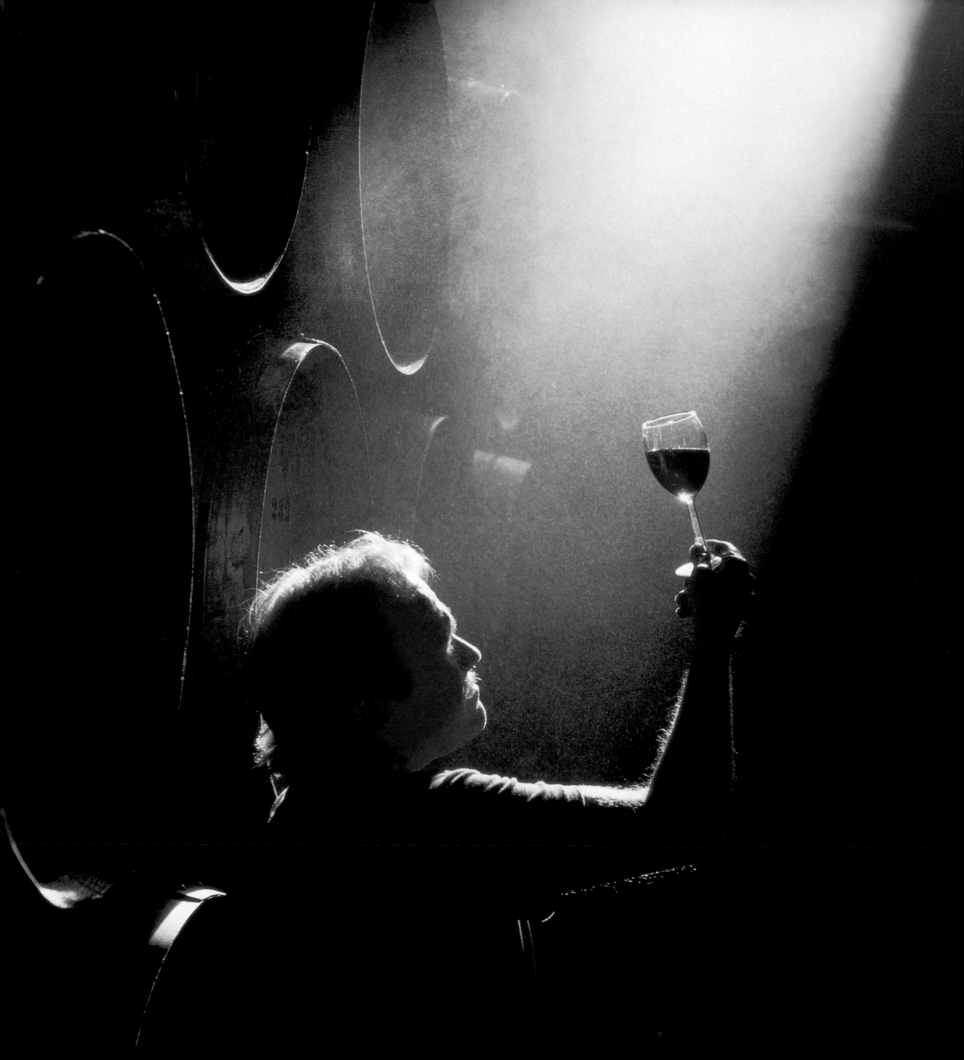

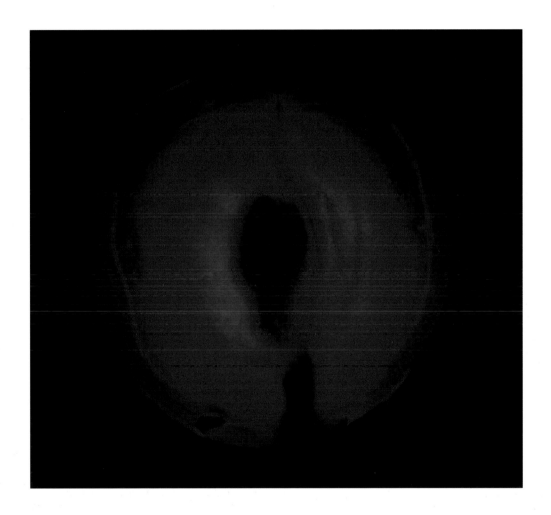

California winemaker Dennis Johns holds a glass in a shaft of sunlight to examine the color
and clarity of a Cabernet *(left)*. A cabernet berry, sliced in half, exposes its inner structure. Cabernet
grapes contain more seed mass in relationship to pulp than most other popular varietals *(above)*.
The family cellar in the tunnels at Beringer Vineyards, St. Helena, California *(following page)*.

"The merest whiff of its aristocratic concentration of blackcurrants and cedar-wood is enough to signal connoisseurs the world over that they are home."

JANCIS ROBINSON
BRITISH WINE AUTHOR

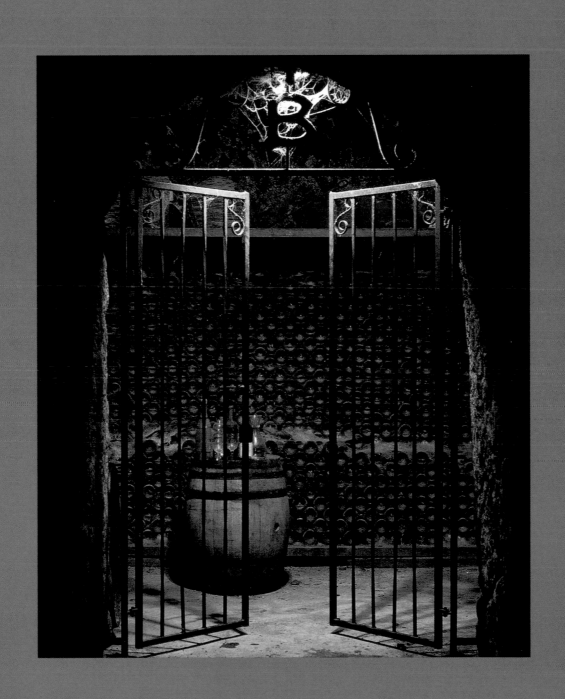

chapter two

CABERNET

the grape

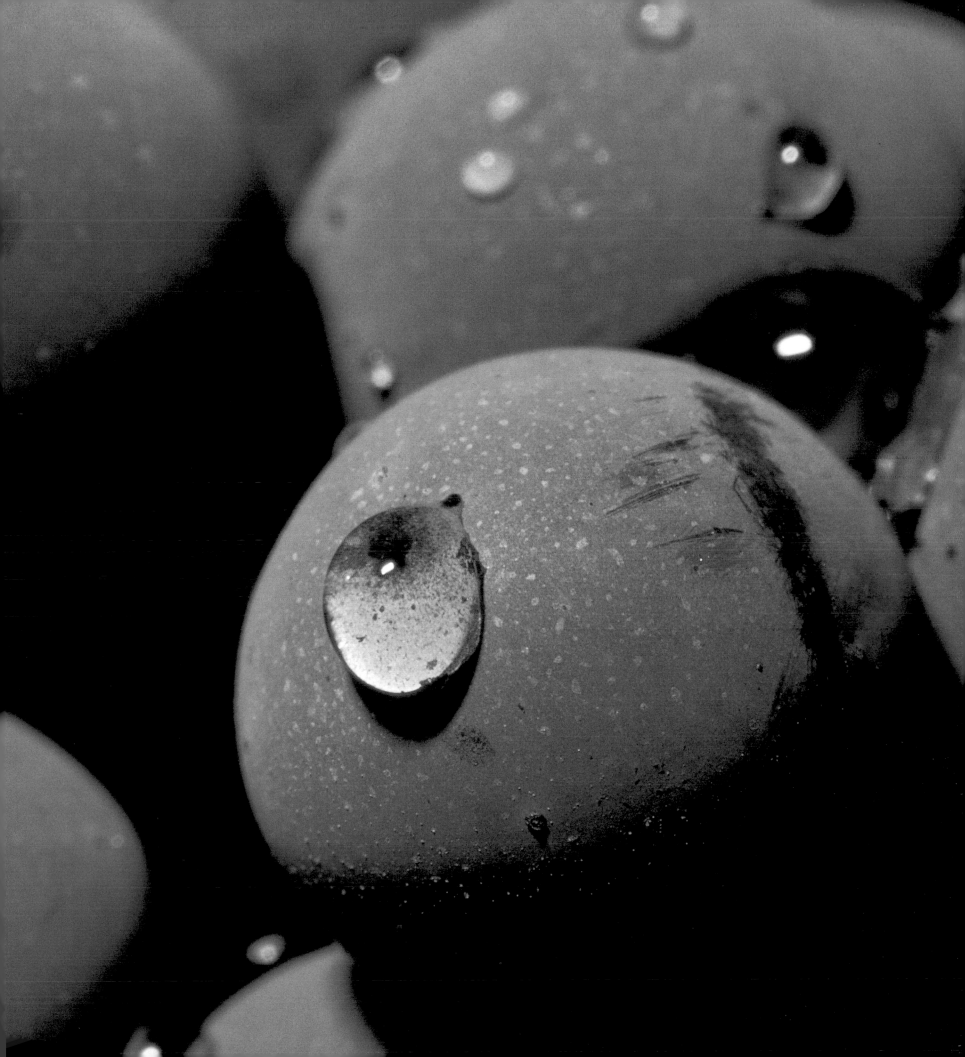

In the kingdom of the vine, cabernet is the grape that most dependably produces great wines. That's not to say that all Cabernets are great wines, of course. For just as a rough diamond needs expert cutting to bring out its brilliance, even vines with noble ancestry like cabernet sauvignon need the hands of a master to produce great wine.

The cabernet vine is among the hardiest in the world. It can resist the heat of South Africa, the cold mornings of Australia, the rains of Bordeaux, and the endless tourists in Napa Valley.

The grape itself is a model of ruggedness. It has a thick tough skin that defies some of the insect pests that bedevil less vigorous varietals and is more resistant to rot.

In France, the motherland of cabernet, the growing environment for wine grapes is known as the *terroir* (pronounced tehr-wah'). It's generally understood to include a vineyard's unique combination of climate, exposure to the sun and wind, and characteristics of its soil and water. There's a great deal of controversy over exactly how much the *terroir* dictates the quality of the resulting wine, but just about everyone agrees that good Cabernet Sauvignon comes only from vineyards that have a temperate climate, adequate sunshine, and soil that's well drained and not too fertile. Premium vineyards are not found side by side with truck farms and fields of corn.

With the growing popularity of premium wine, including Cabernet, the land devoted to grapes worldwide is increasing rapidly. Planting in a new vineyard or replanting with new vines is a major undertaking. After the land is prepared by clearing trees and plants, the vines must be planted. That requires putting in a rootstock that is resistant to *phylloxera*, a small root-feeding louse that was responsible for destroying the entire European and California wine industry in the late nineteenth century and then struck California again almost a century later.

In some regions of Bordeaux, a vine may produce enough grapes for only half a bottle of wine. Elsewhere a cabernet vine might produce five or ten times as much. There is a theory that the best wines come from vines with the least fruit on them. Vines that are heavily watered and fertilized certainly don't produce high-quality grapes because the flavors in the juice are less concentrated. But adding to the enigmatic nature of winemaking, some of the finest Cabernet wines have been produced during years that also produced the most abundant harvests.

Making great wine is more than merely finding a good plot of land and planting grapes that come from good parents. Viticulture is a year-round job that involves pruning and training the vines, weeding the grounds, watering at the right time, treating for insects and mold, and protecting against birds, animals, and other hazards.

In order to harvest grapes that have the flavor and sugar content that's needed to make great wine, the grower has to make a number of critical decisions. Among those are how much to irrigate and at what time in the growing cycle, how much to thin the developing clusters of grapes, and how to train the vines.

By the time the grapes are approaching maturity in late summer or early fall, the important preparations have been completed and all that's left is the absolutely critical step of picking the grapes exactly when the time is right.

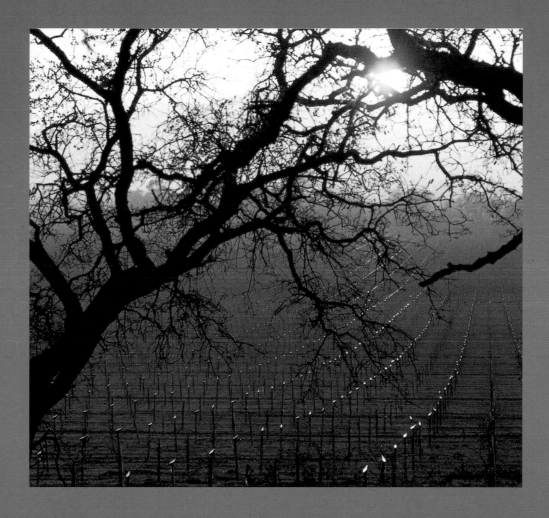

Morning dew highlights a cabernet grape that is only days
from achieving full ripeness *(preceding pages)*. The distant light of the sun brings
scant warmth to dormant vines in a California vineyard *(above)*.

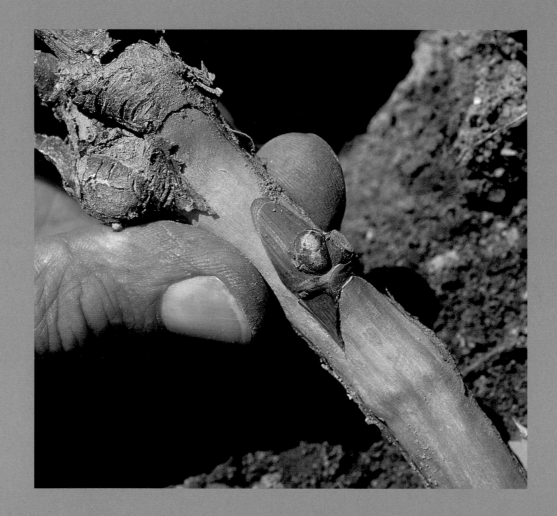

Work in the vineyard never ends. New cabernet buds are grafted to rootstock in the fall before the vines become dormant *(above)*. In the Médoc region in France workers prune back vines in winter to promote vigorous new growth in the springtime *(right)*.

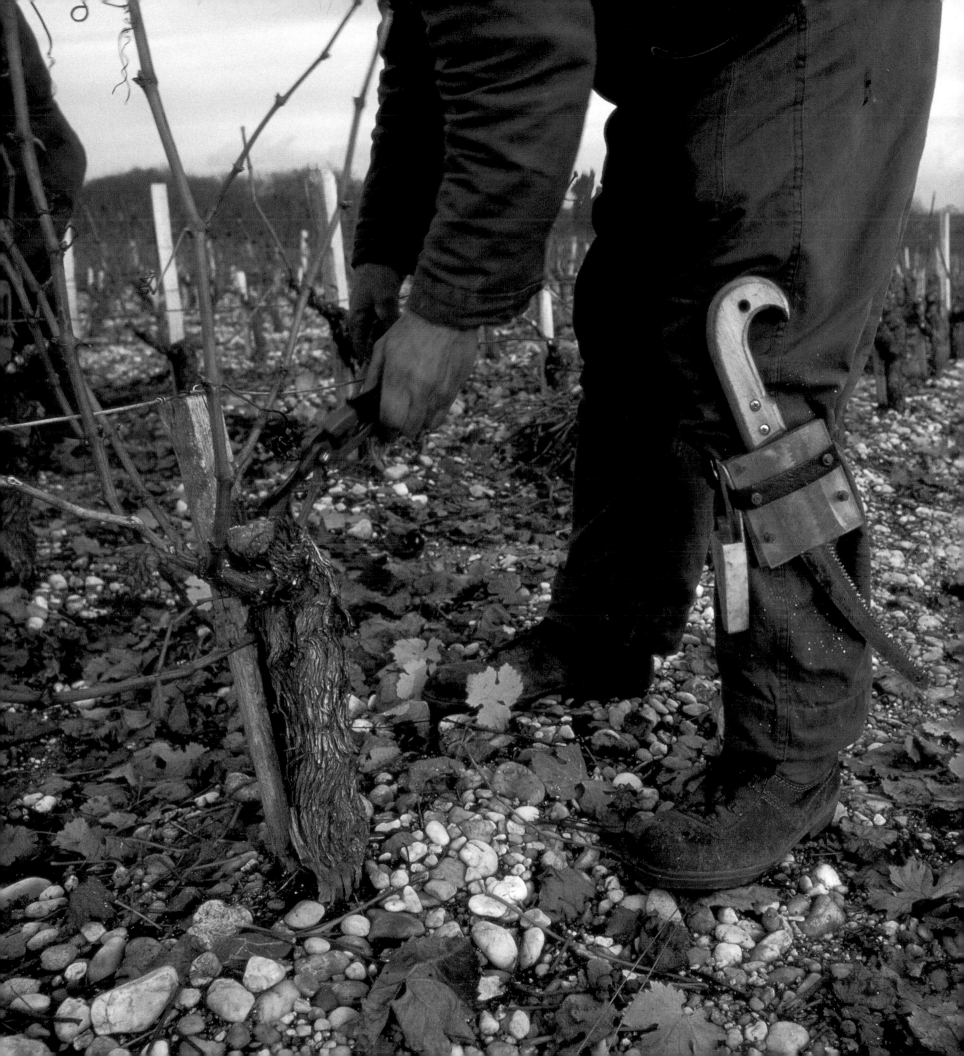

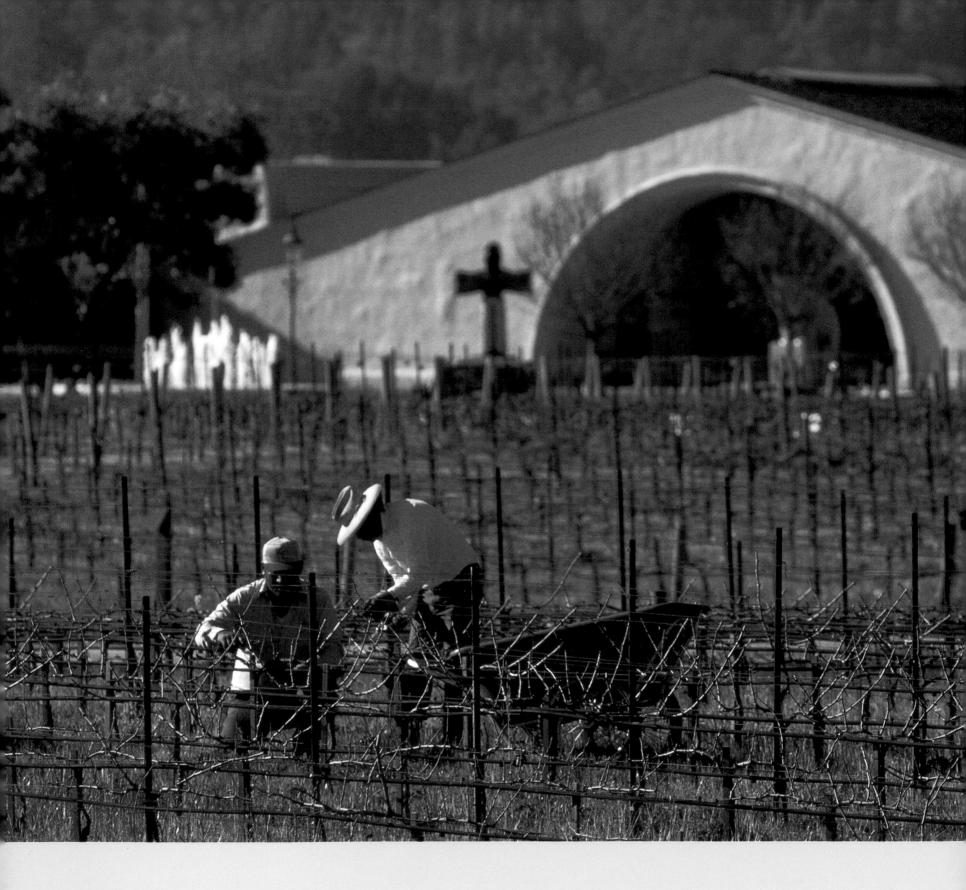

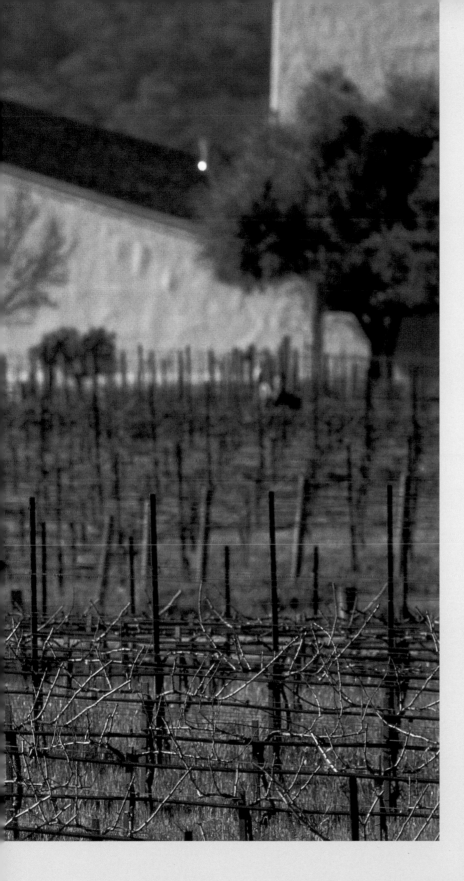

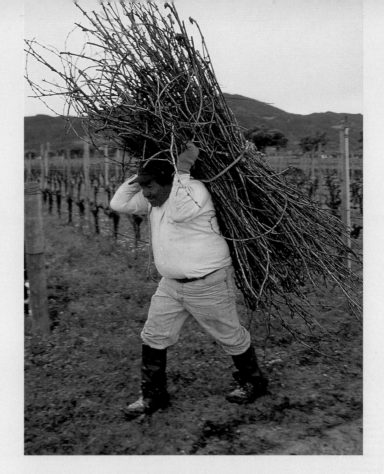

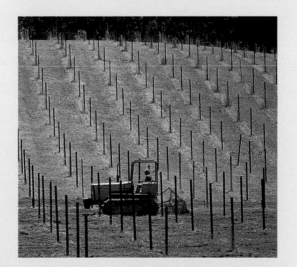

california

Wineries established in the valleys that twine through the mediterranean climate north of San Francisco have earned a reputation for excellent Cabernet. In all of California, more than 400 wineries make wine with cabernet grapes. Workers prune vines in front of the Robert Mondavi Winery in Oakville *(left)*. A vineyard helper at Opus One carries away a heavy load of vines *(top)*. More cabernet grapes will soon grow on this newly prepared plot in the Napa Valley *(above)*.

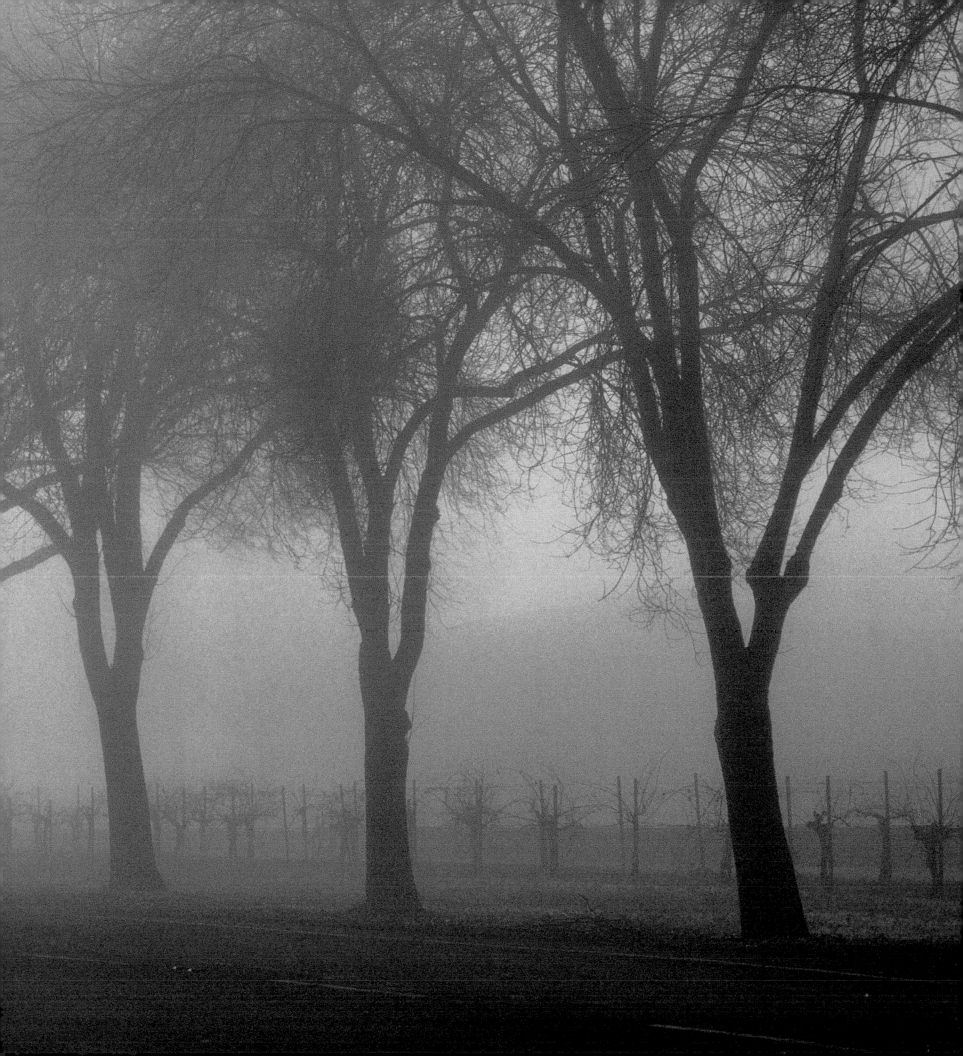

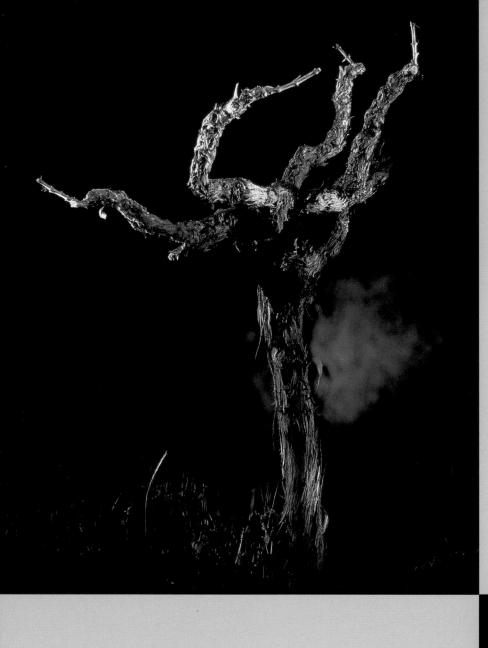

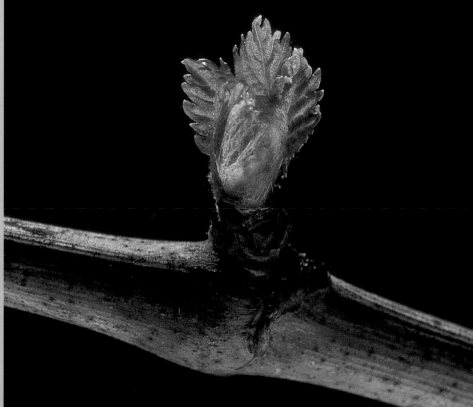

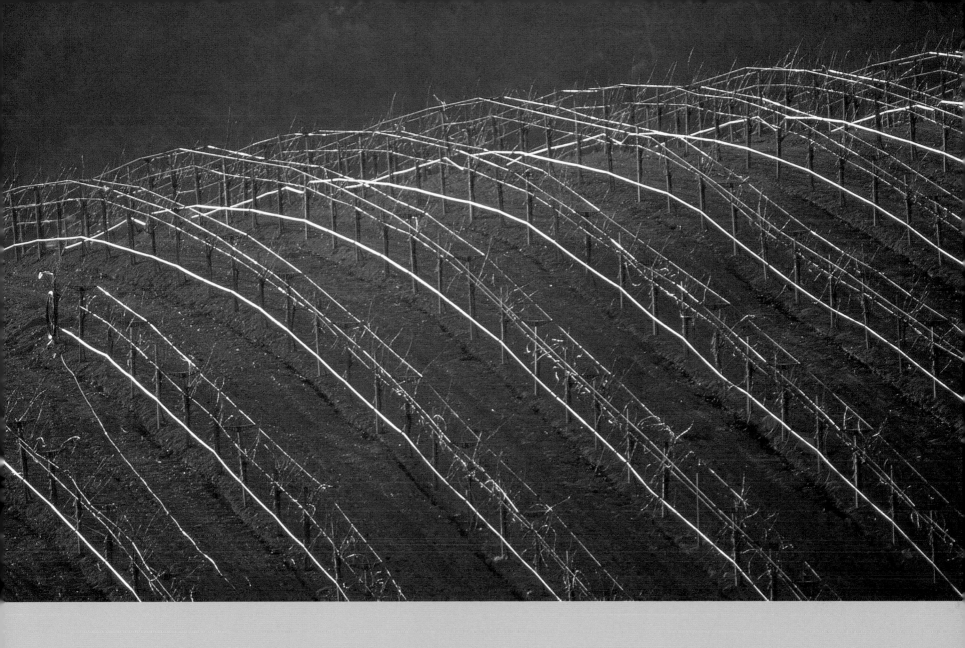

Winter fog on Highway 29 in Rutherford, California, lies like a blanket over dormant vines *(preceding pages)*.
Like a dancer, a dormant vine sways gracefully in the winter wind *(top left)*. A bud emerges from a cane in early spring, already
carrying microscopic berries that will mature in a full cluster of grapes within six months *(left)*. Drip irrigation pipes near Napa,
which will water the vines during summer, reflect the winter sunrise *(above)*.

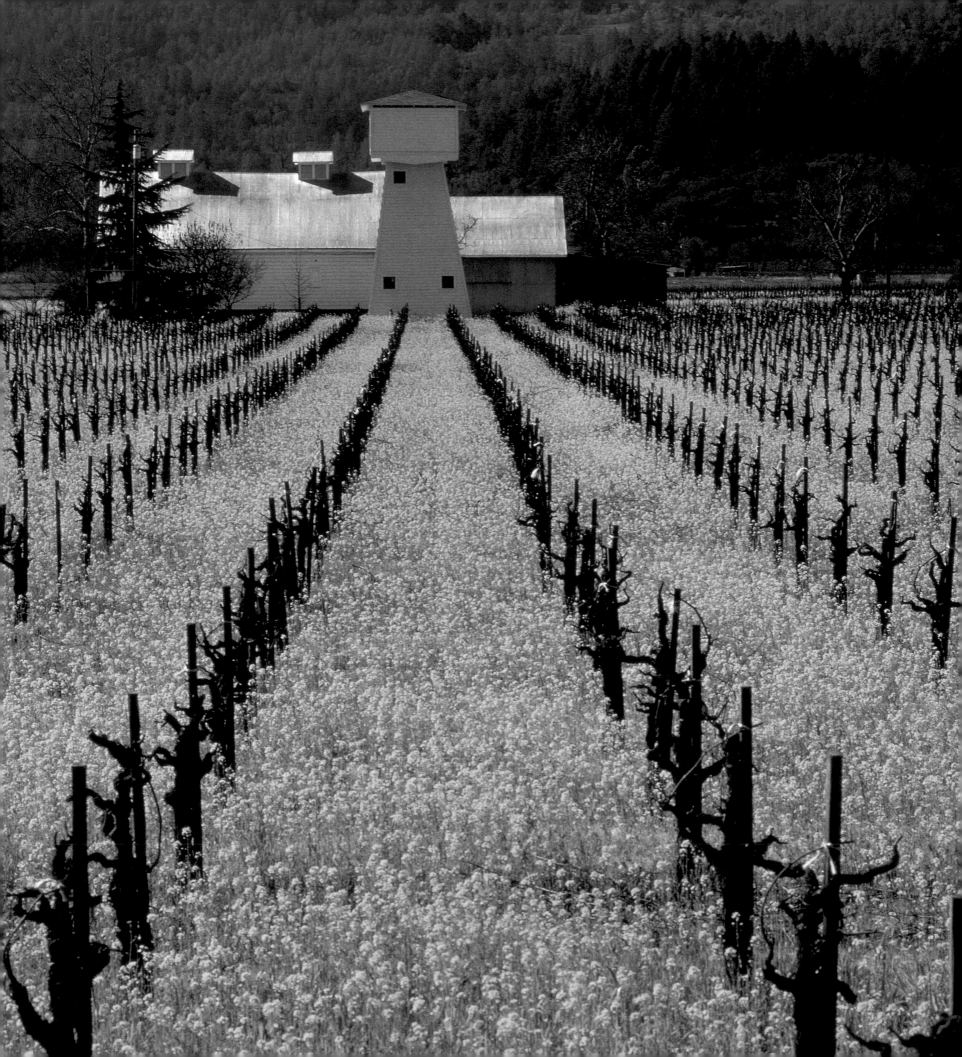

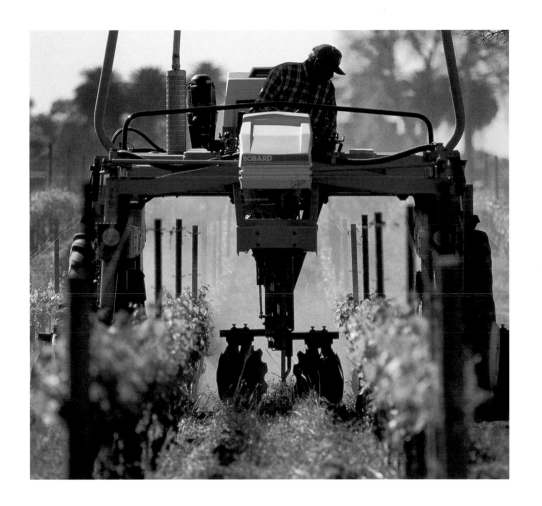

Colorful mustard weeds in a Napa Valley vineyard *(left)* will be plowed under before
the dormant vines awaken. Although a springtime signal of the start of the growing season,
weeds steal moisture and nutrients from the vines. A French-made tractor finds
a home in an Oakville, California, vineyard *(above)*. It straddles two rows of vines and is
an important tool in cultivating the increasingly popular, densely planted vineyards.

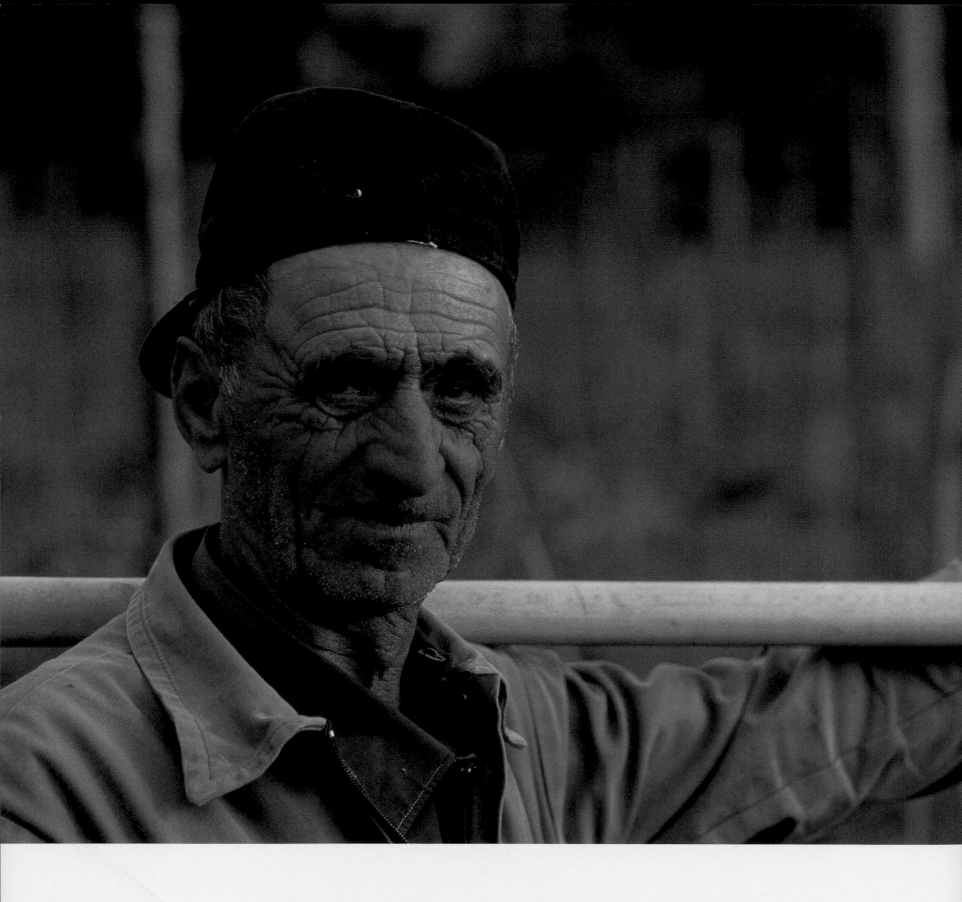

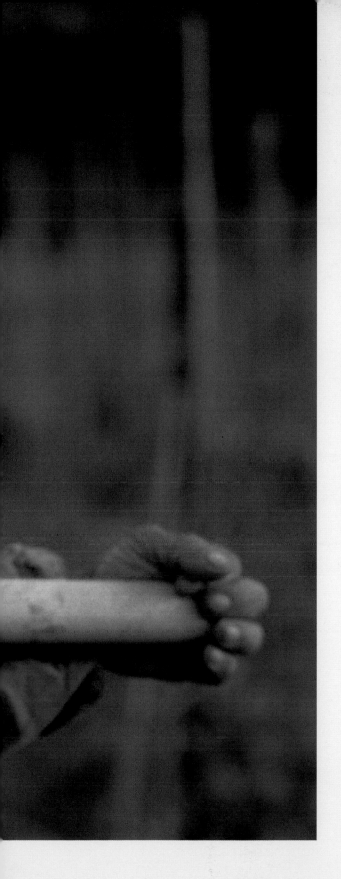

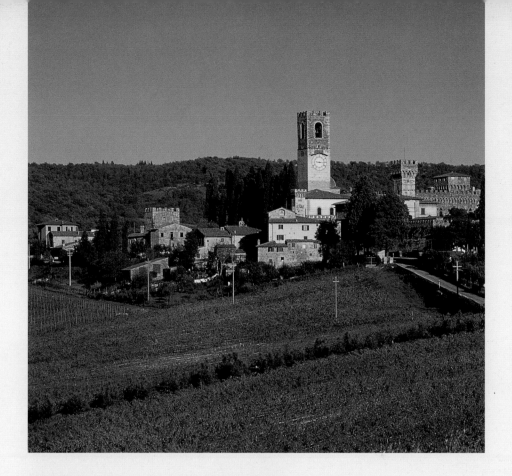

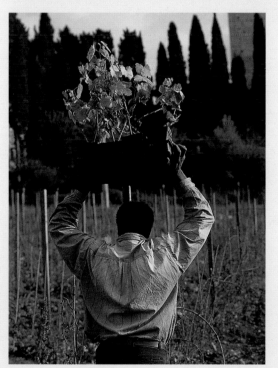

italy

A vineyard worker in the Tuscany region of Italy stakes out rows of a new vineyard *(left)*. In the village of

Passignano, a monastery tower becomes a landmark in this grape-growing region south of Florence *(top)*.

The vines being planted in this Italian vineyard began in a nursery and after planting

will produce grapes in two years, a year sooner than vines that are field-grafted *(above)*.

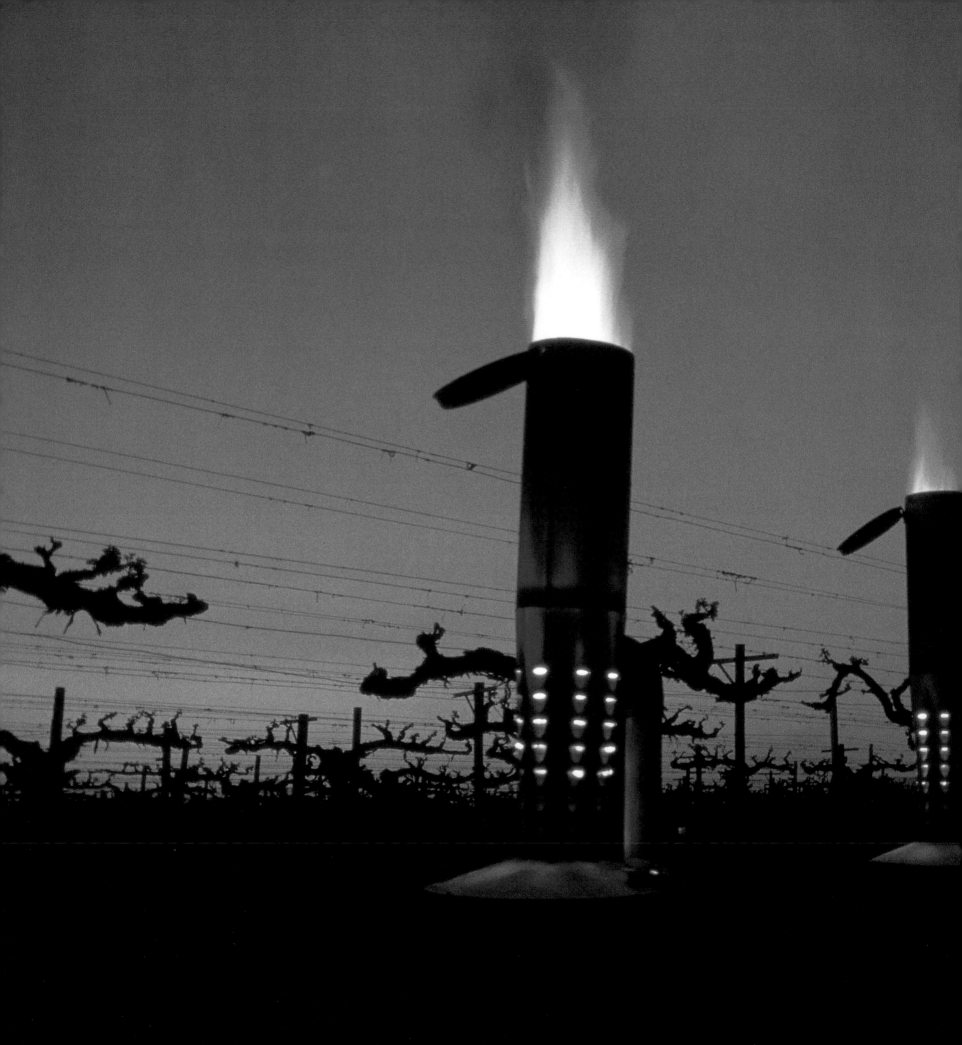

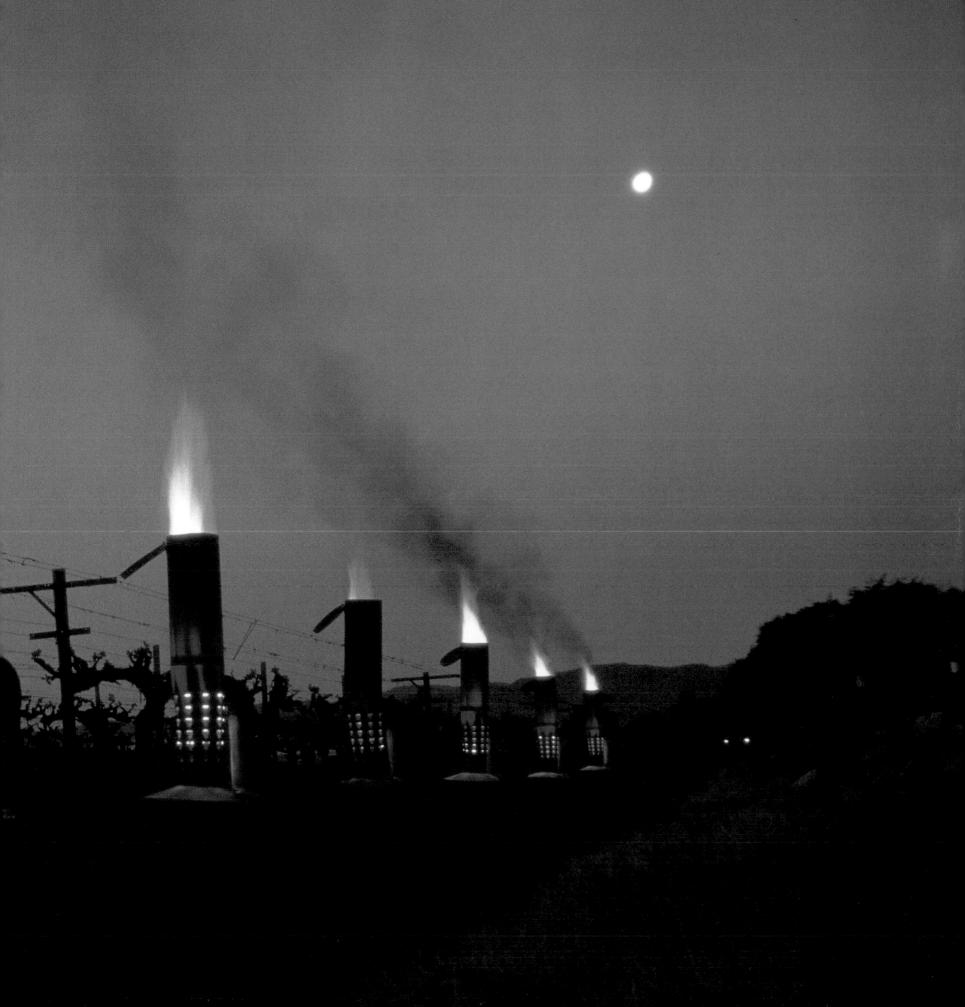

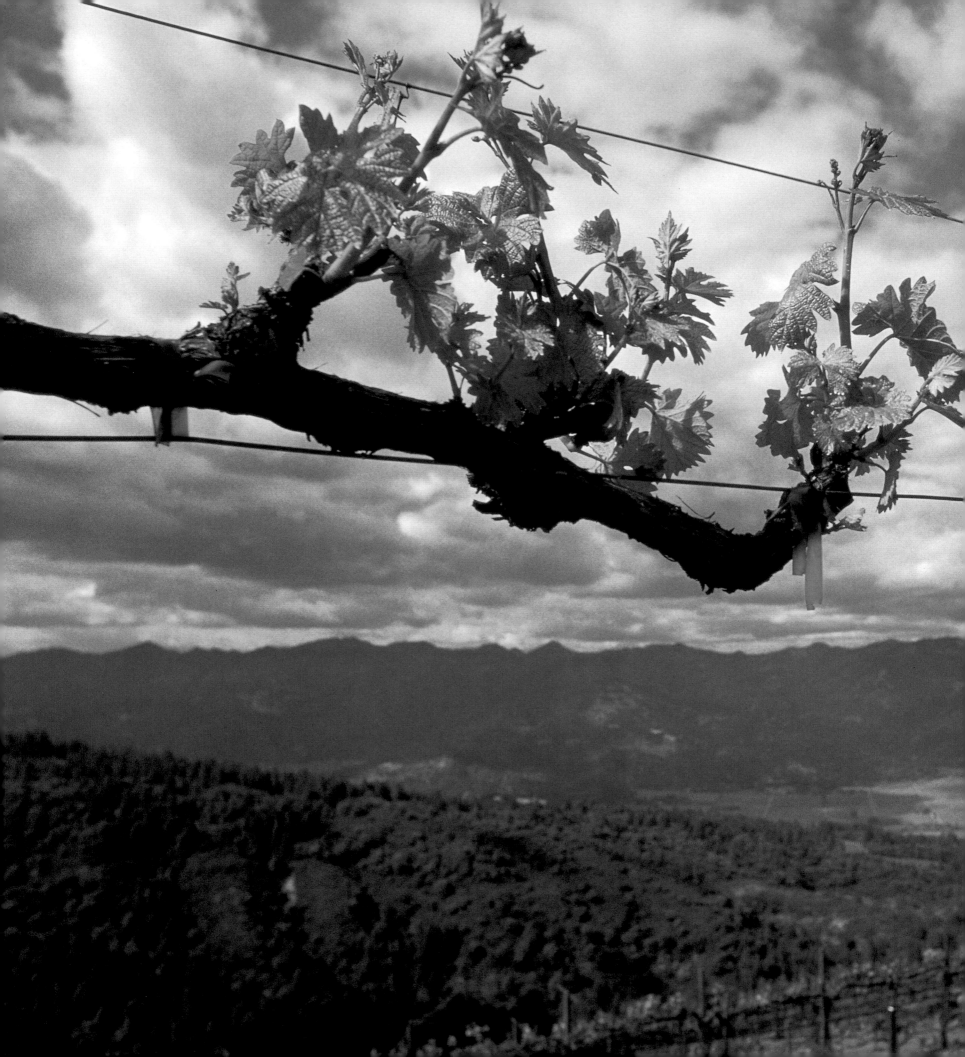

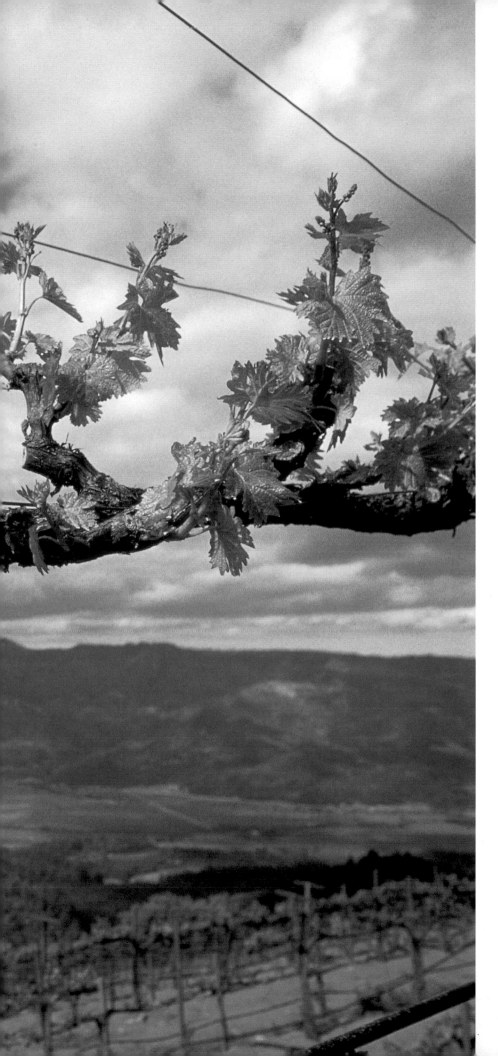

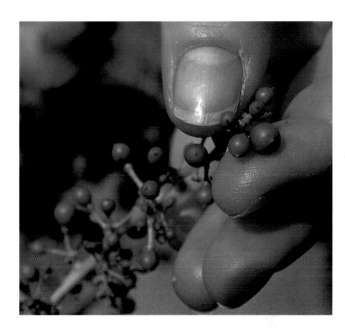

Vineyards become vulnerable to frost damage
when tender young shoots appear in the spring. At Stag's Leap
Wine Cellars, near Napa, California, *(preceding pages)* orchard
heaters are fired just before sunrise. When oil-burning
heaters are fully warmed up, their lids will be closed to radiate
heat outward into the vines. The fragile buds on these
trellised vines are still susceptible to damage from frost *(left)*.
Delicate new flowers on the cabernet vine will set fruit
in just a few weeks *(above)*.

65

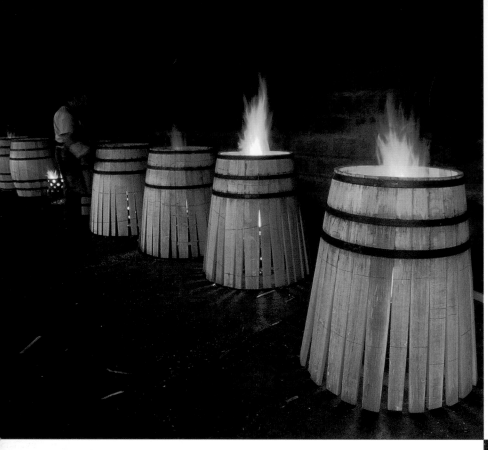

As grapes ripen in the fields, other vital facets of the winemaking process proceed at full speed. In barrel factories called cooperages, flames provide the heat that softens water-soaked oak staves so they can be bent into tight barrels *(above)*. Expensive oak barrels sometimes are reconditioned by shaving a thin layer from the inside. Because the flavor of wine is significantly influenced by the type of wood used and the degree to which the interior is charred, reconditioned barrels are almost never used for premium cabernet *(right)*. At Demptos, near Bordeaux, a workman selects willow bark which will wrap a decorative rim on barrels *(above right)*. The wood around this barrel's opening, known as the bunghole, is stained red because the wine is sampled or transferred through this opening many times during the aging process *(far right)*.

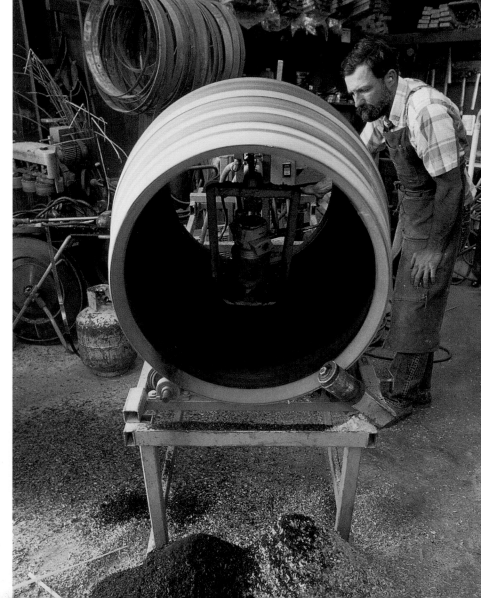

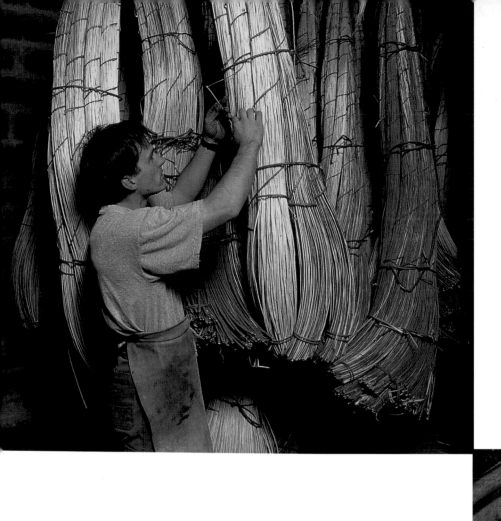

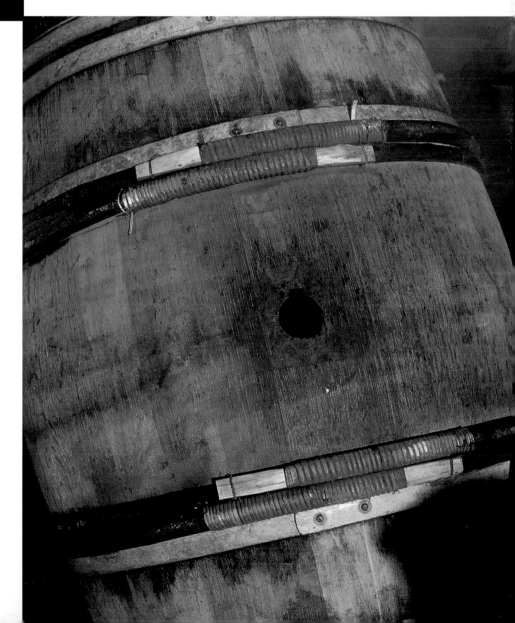

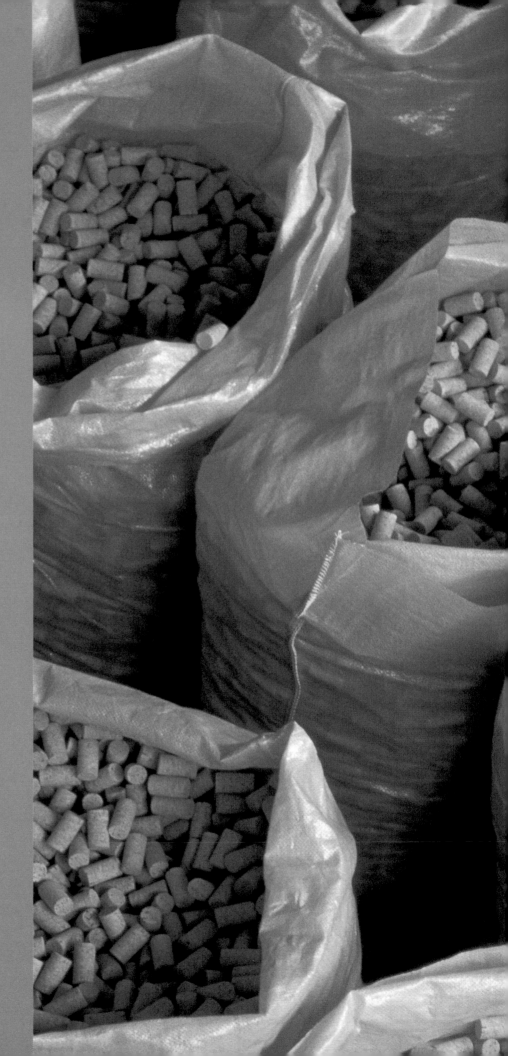

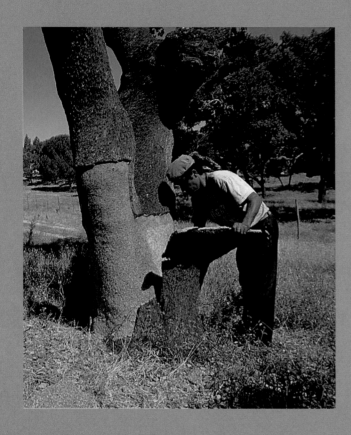

Most of the corks that secure Cabernet in bottles
come from trees in Portugal, the world's leading supplier.
A craftsman strips thick bark from a Mediterranean
oak tree near Lisbon *(above)*. The bark grows back to harvest
thickness in nine years. Cork stoppers have sealed
wine bottles for centuries, and despite numerous lower cost
alternatives, the mystique of fine Cabernet demands it
always be sealed with cork. Corks punched from sheets of
boiled oak bark await shipment in a Porto cork processing
plant *(right)*. At sunset, a Tuscan farmer in Passignano
returns from his vineyards *(following page)*.

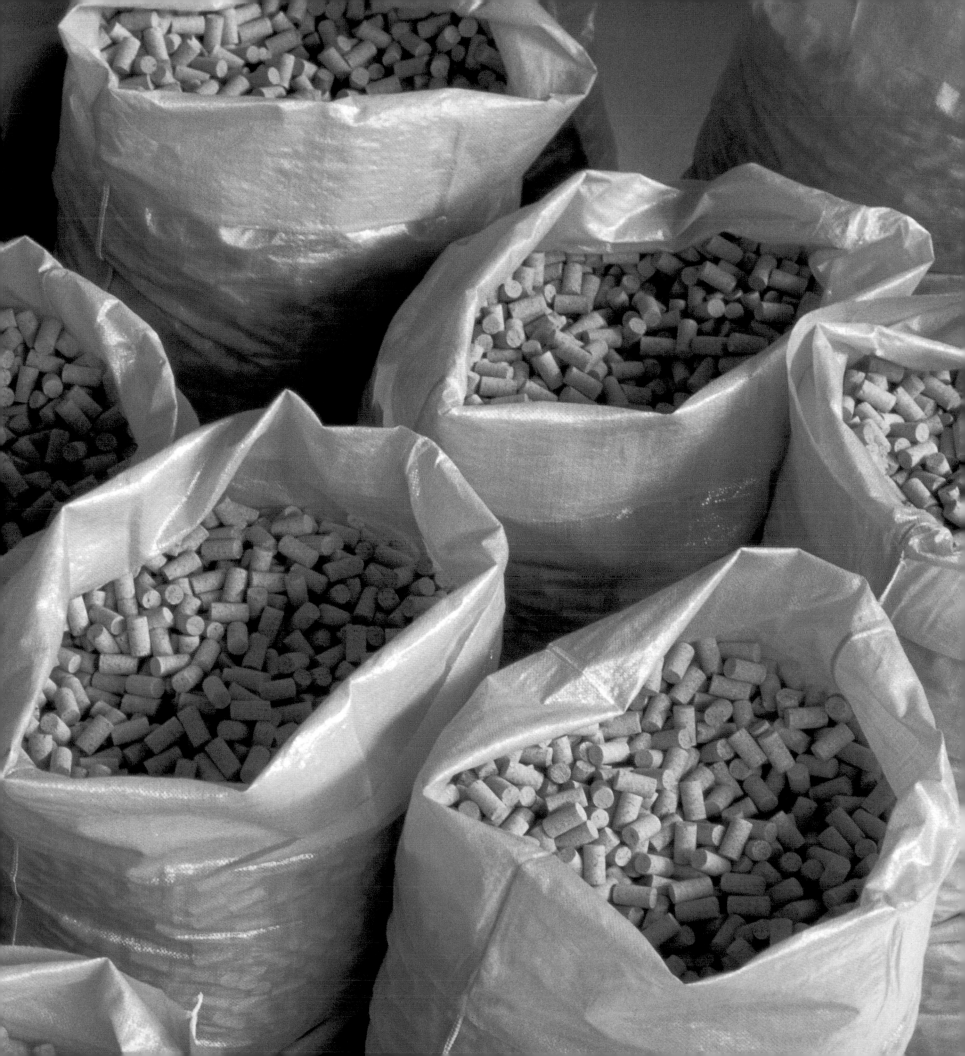

PETER HØJ

DIRECTOR, AUSTRALIAN WINE RESEARCH INSTITUTE AND PROFESSOR OENOLOGY,
THE UNIVERSITY OF ADELAIDE, AUSTRALIA

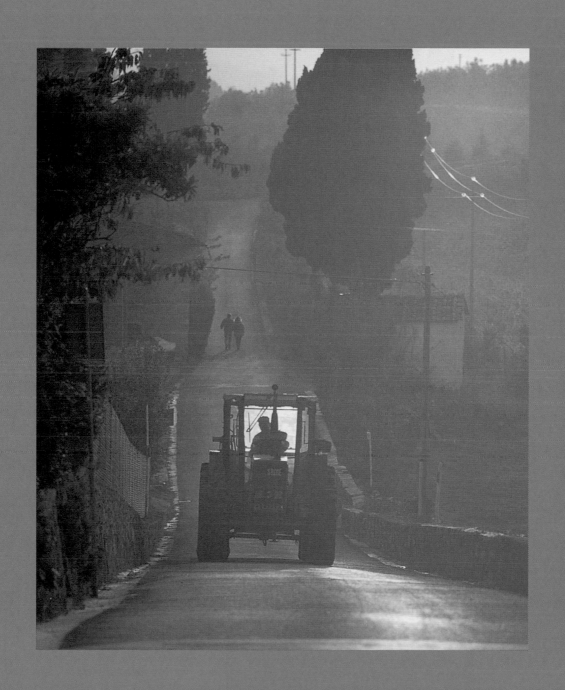

chapter three

CABERNET

the harvest

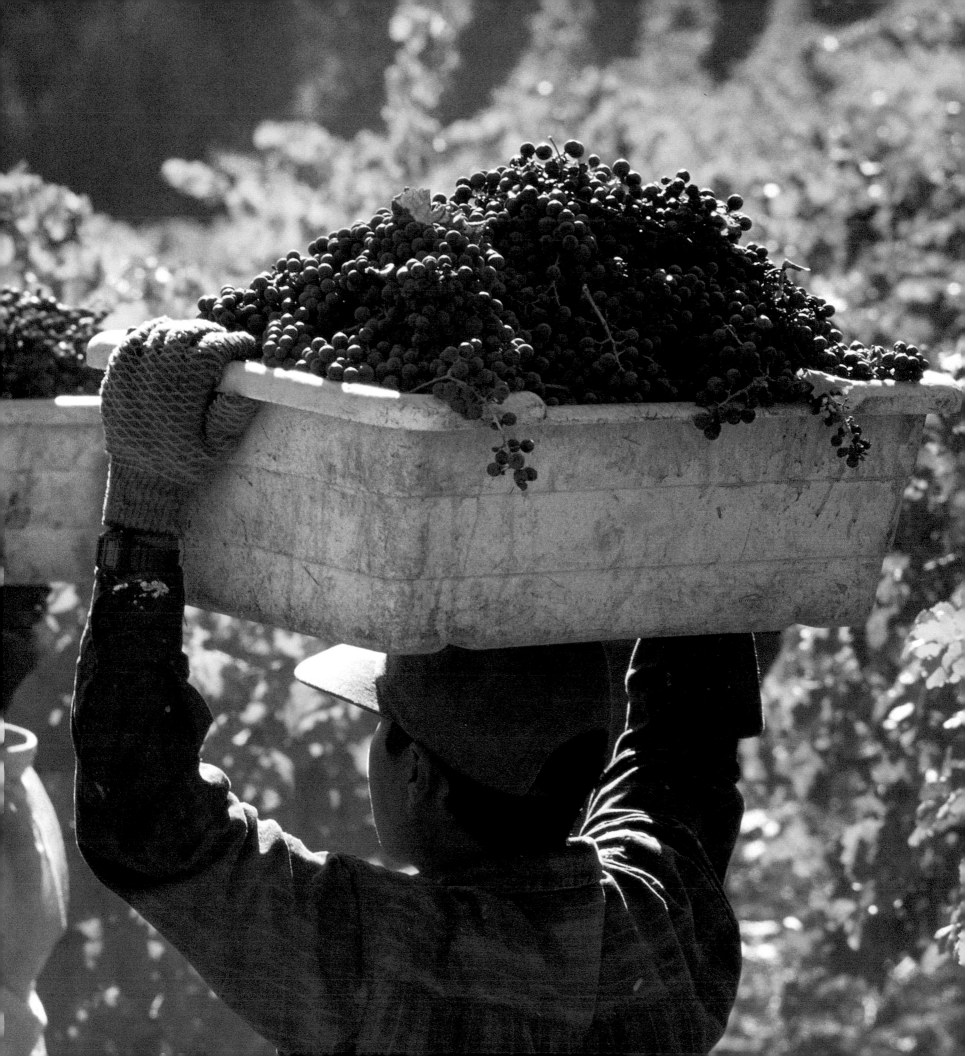

Harvest time in the wine country is like the Super Bowl, Election Day, and final exams all at once.

It's a time of very hard work and frantic activity.

It's an anxious time of wondering about the quality of wine the grapes will produce.

And at the end, when the last grapes have come in from the field, it's a happy celebration of nature's bounty, for harvest is the climax of everything for which the growers have been planning, paying, and praying.

Deciding when to pick the grapes is the most critical judgment that will determine the wine's quality. If picked too early, the grapes won't have reached their peak of sugar and flavor. If the grapes are picked too late, fungus, plant viruses, or a storm may cripple the harvest.

It's during harvest that the viticulture experiments conducted by the growers during the previous year receive their final grades. Did spacing the grapevines further apart really increase quality? Did training the vines on wire trellises increase production? How much was quality improved by midsummer irrigation?

Another factor that affects the quality of the finished wine is the way the grapes are picked and handled. Harvesting for premium wines like Cabernet is still almost always done by hand. Mechanical picking machines can be used for clearing the vines of ordinary wine grapes but are seldom used for fine vintages.

A good handpicker, using a curved knife or specialized clippers, can harvest as much as two tons of grapes a day, equal to 126 cases of finished wine. Once the grapes are hauled from the field into the winery, they are quickly dumped into a machine that separates the berries from the stems. It also gently crushes the grapes but doesn't damage the seeds, which are bitter on the inside.

The crushed grape and juice mixture is called "must." In making red wines like Cabernet Sauvignon, the natural yeasts and bacteria of the grape are usually killed with a diluted solution of sulfur dioxide. Then a carefully selected strain of yeast is added to begin fermentation. A hard cap of skins and stems floats to the surface as the yeast converts the sugar in the juice into alcohol. The cap helps control the amount of oxygen that gets into the fermenting mixture, but it must be broken up and the fermenting juice pumped over it frequently. That contact between juice and skins is needed to extract the tannins that provide the wine with color, flavor, and longevity.

Finally, a few weeks after the grapes have been picked from the vines, the juice has been magically transformed into young wine. It is pumped into barrels for aging and often a secondary fermentation.

The harvest is over. Workers and growers breath a sigh of relief and then celebrate. But the final grades on this vintage still won't be known for several more years until aging and some very careful blending have occured.

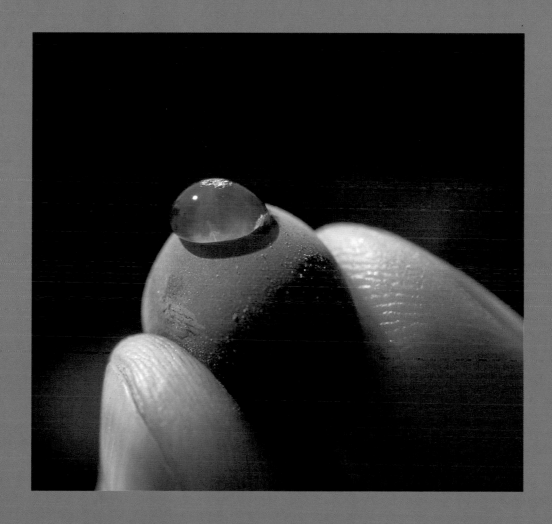

Pickers wait patiently for a wheeled "gondola" that will take these cabernet grapes from
their overloaded boxes to the winery *(preceding pages)*. The fingers of a Chilean vineyard manager
pinch a grape and determine from the feel that picking begins tomorrow *(above)*.

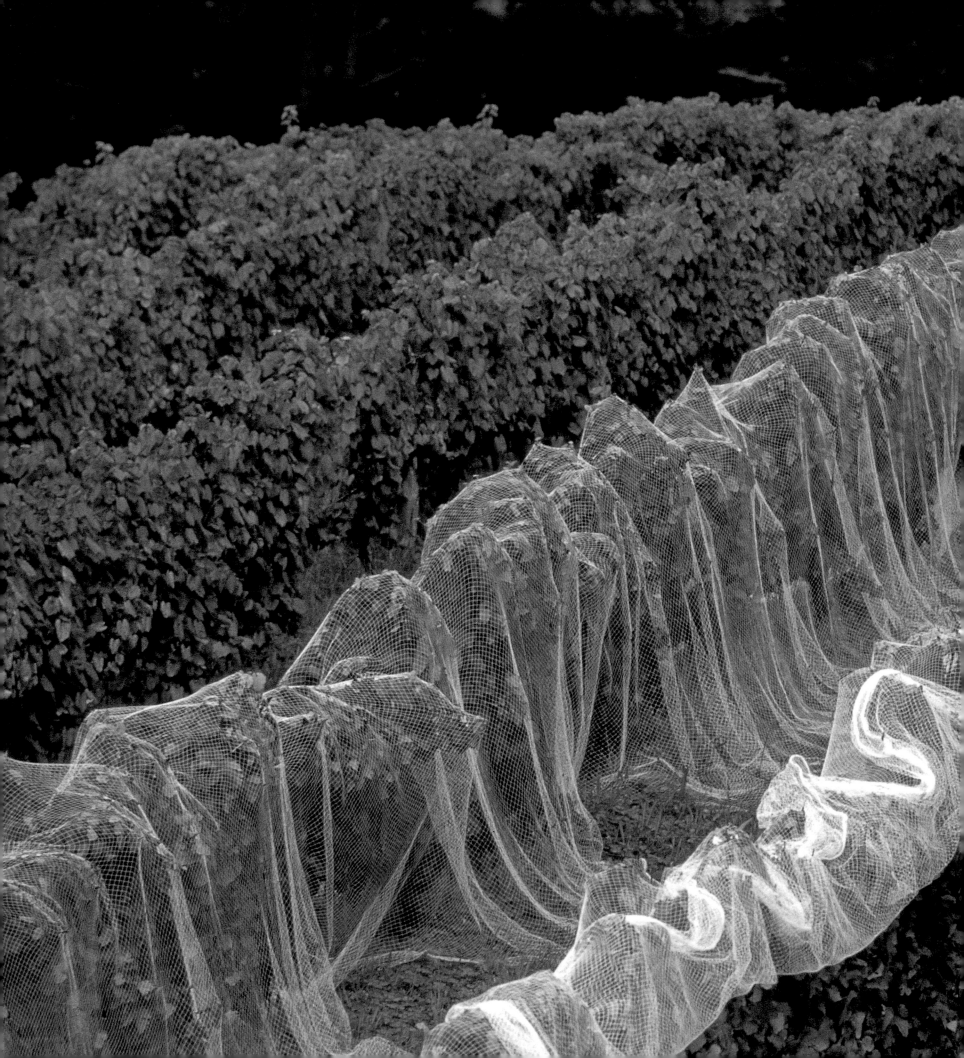

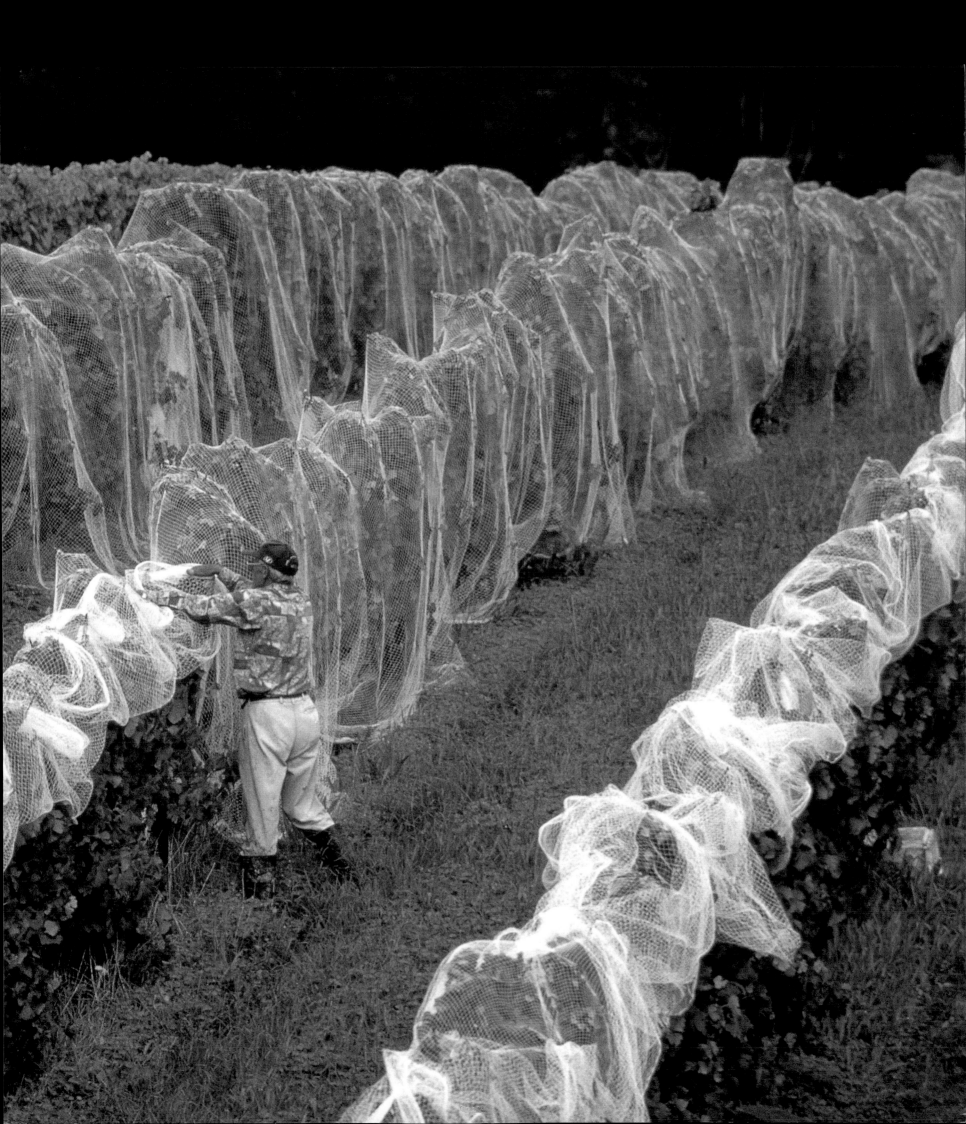

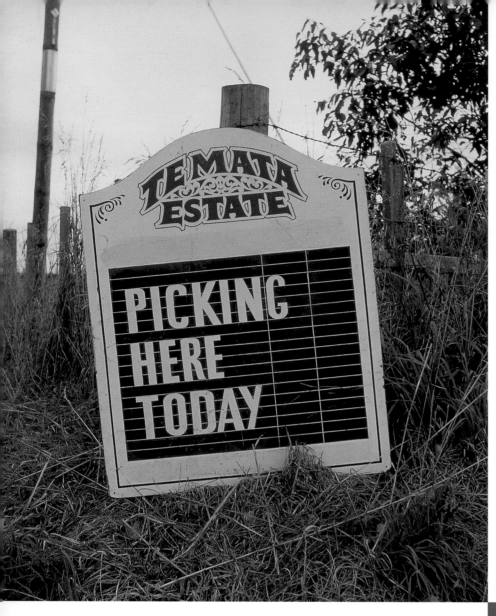

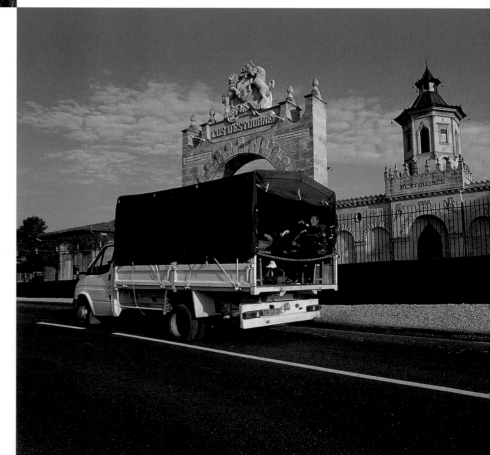

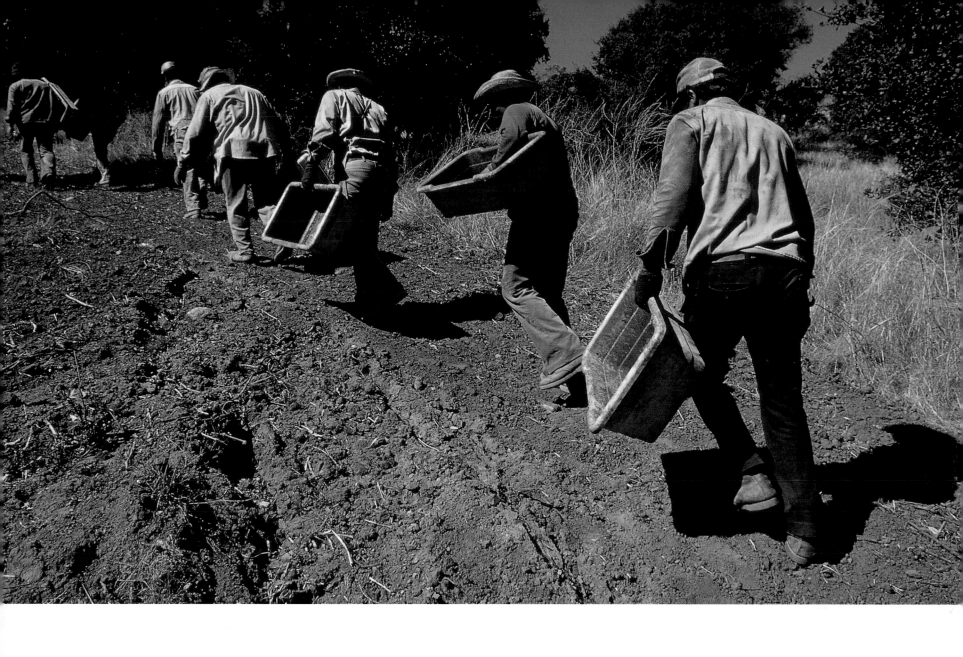

Preparing for a New Zealand harvest, a worker lifts the skirts of bird netting at a vineyard near
Auckland *(preceding pages)*. The aggressive bird problem is especially severe in New Zealand because nonnative birds,
which have no natural enemies, have multiplied to a point where tight mesh netting is needed even when
the grapes are still green. Neighbors of this Hawke's Bay, New Zealand, winery can earn cash picking grapes when the harvest
is ready *(top left)*. A truckload of French pickers drives past Cos d'Estournel in the Médoc region *(left)*. Pickers march up
Diamond Mountain in Napa Valley to harvest hillside-grown cabernet grapes *(above)*.

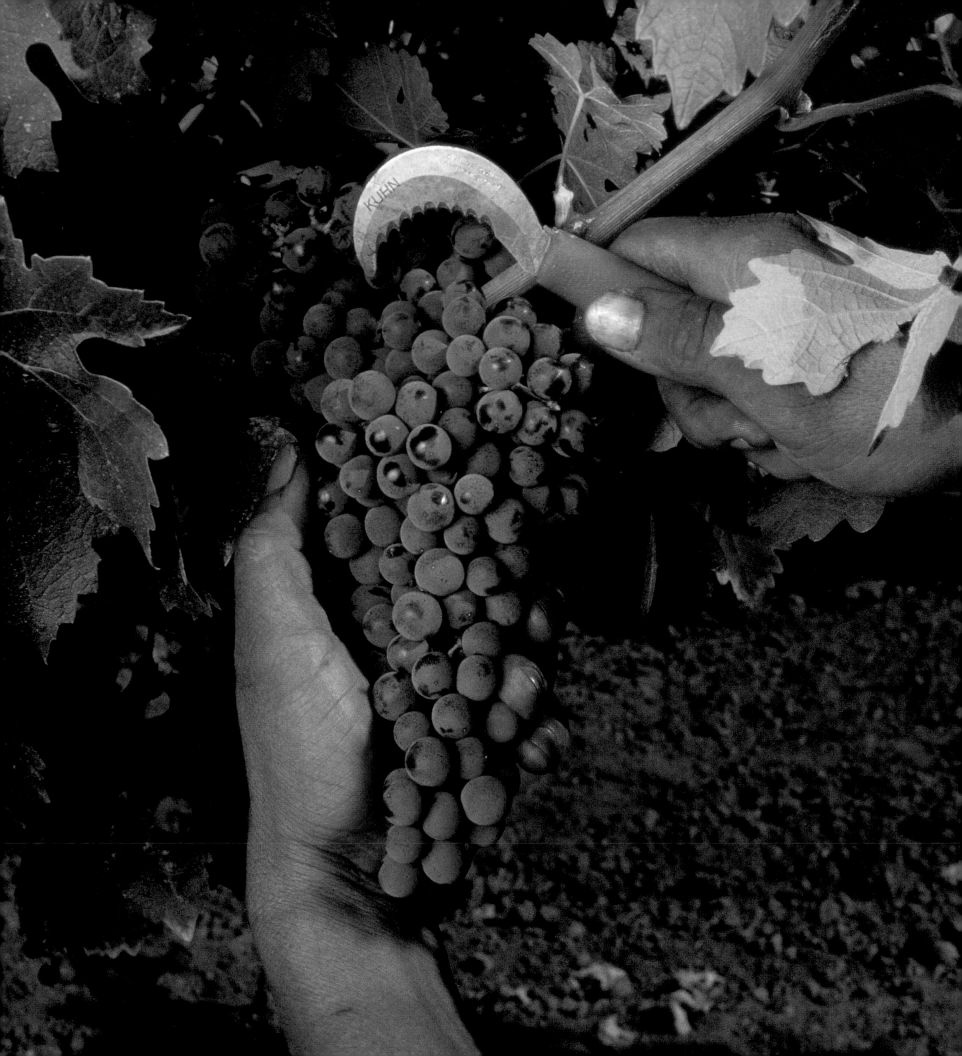

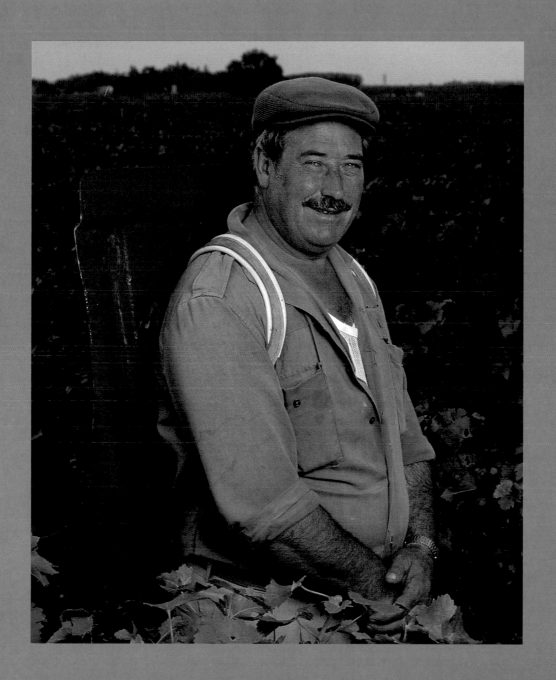

The hooked knife is the preferred personal tool for wine pickers in California *(left)*.
Elsewhere, scissors and snippers are more popular. A picker from a Spanish village near
Jaen poses in a French vineyard with his last load of the day *(above)*.

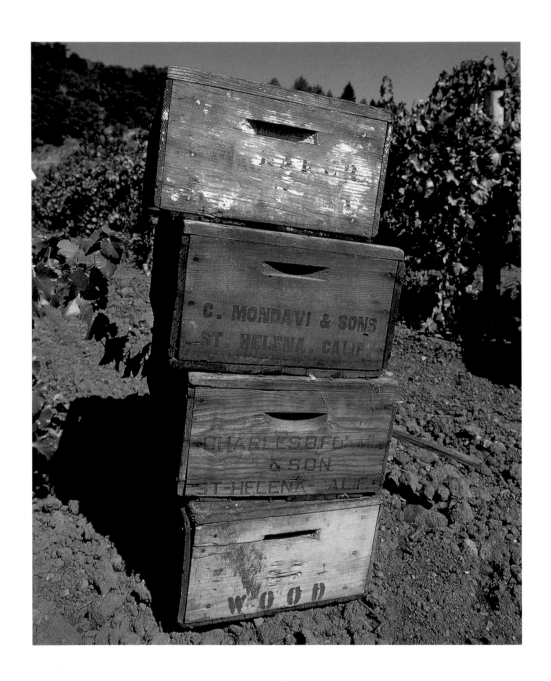

Traditional wood boxes are being replaced by plastic buckets and boxes
that are lighter, stronger, and more easily cleaned helping to prevent mold and
diseases from spreading to the grapes *(above)*. Picking shears that are
provided by the grower await harvesters in the Yarra Valley of Australia *(right)*.

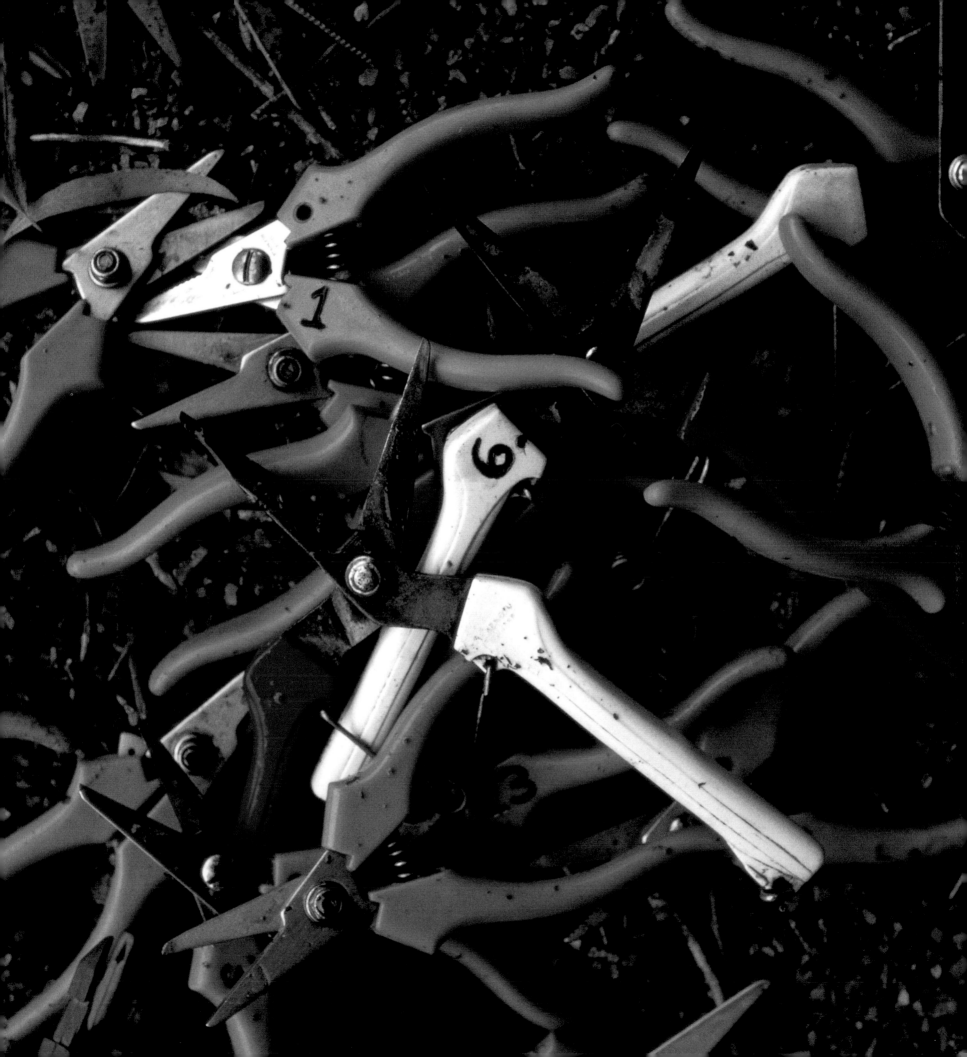

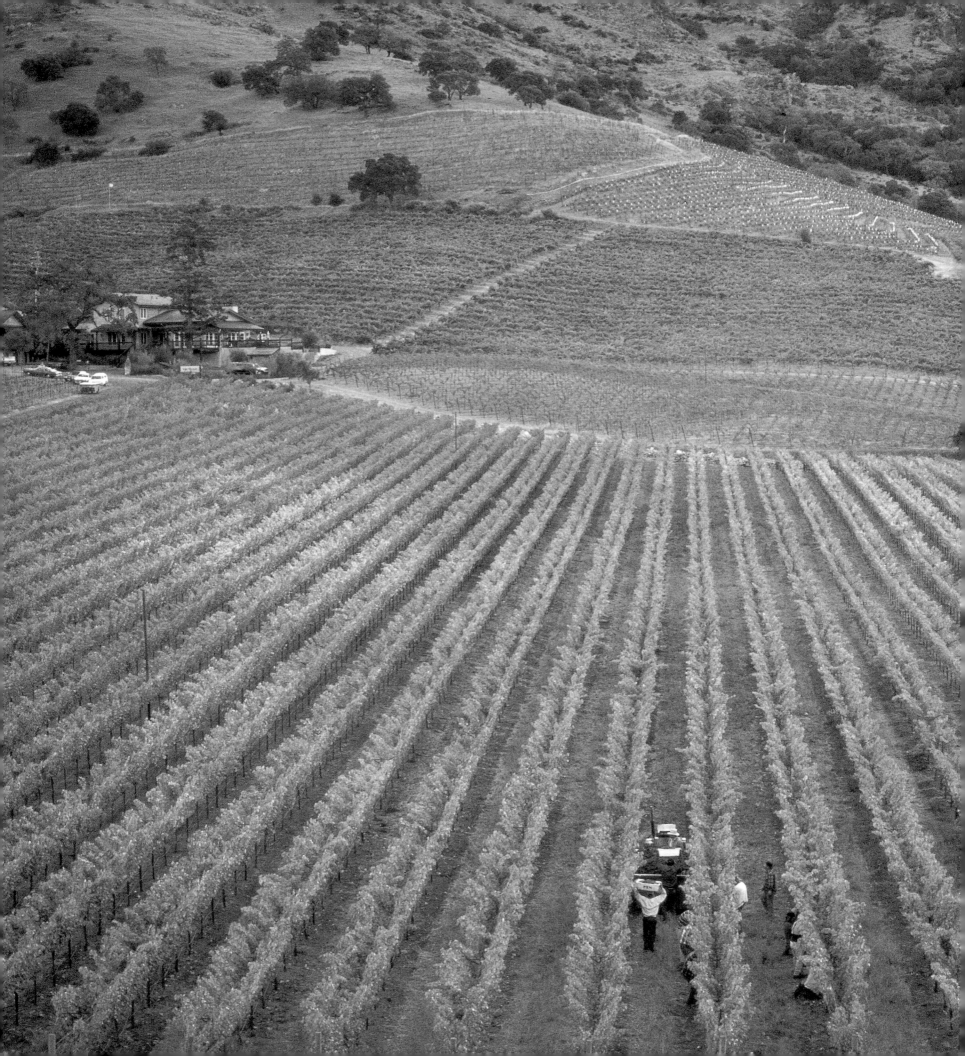

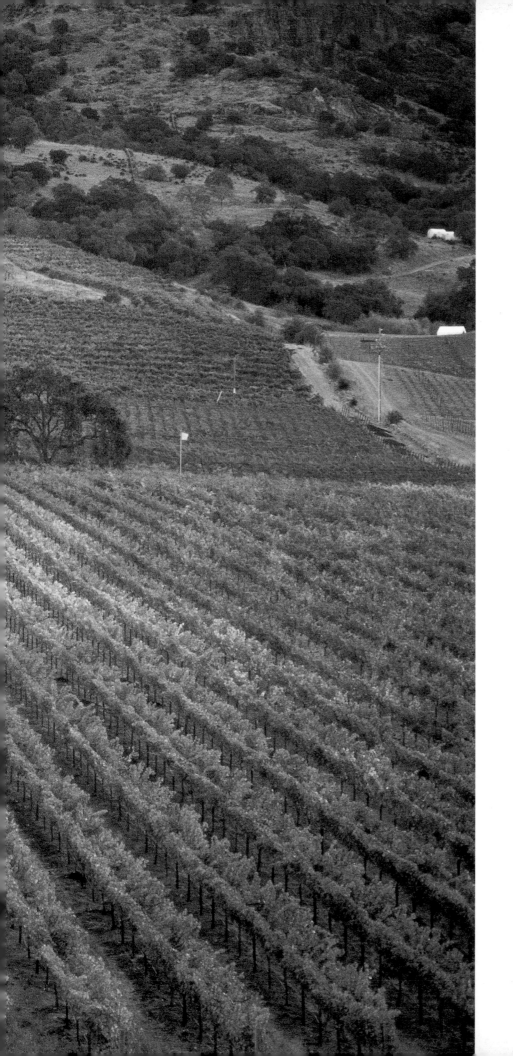

In only a couple of days, a small crew will pick these nine acres of cabernet at Shafer Vineyards in California's Stags Leap district, one of several recognized regions in the Napa Valley. Federal law allows these districts to be identified on labels to give consumers more information about the wine's origin.

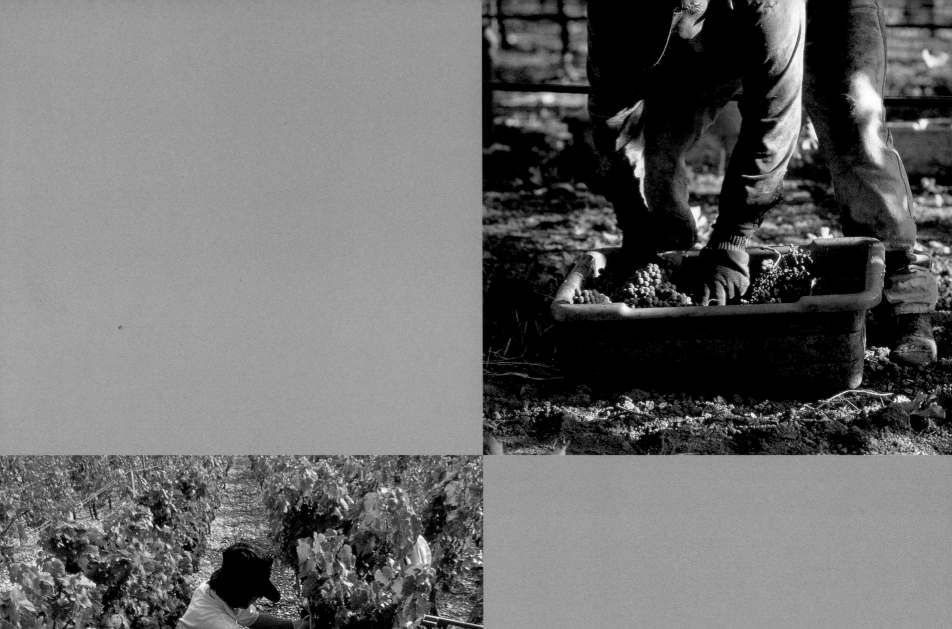

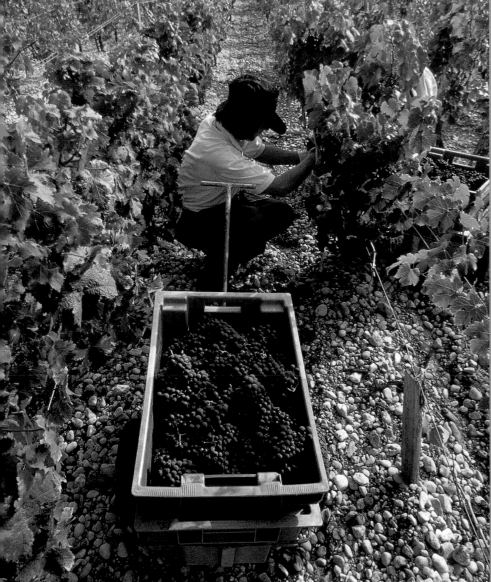

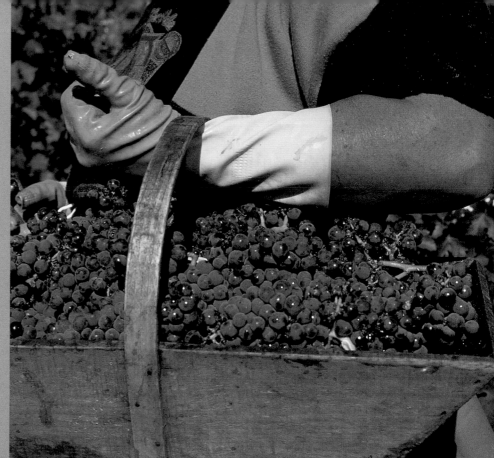

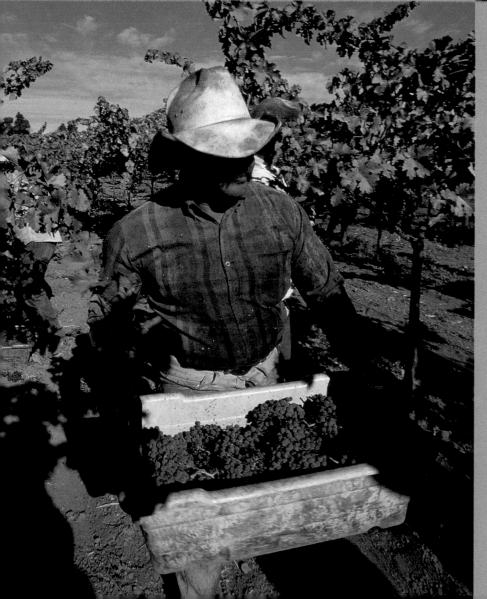

Although mechanized picking is used extensively in the production of *vin ordinaire*, growers of premium quality cabernet sauvignon grapes discourage its use because mechanical picking can bruise the grapes and oxidize the juice. Handpicking is considered gentler and cleaner. Some of the most expensive cabernet grapes on earth get special treatment during harvest at Château Mouton-Rothschild in Bordeaux *(far left)*. Special care in the harvest is also demanded of pickers at Robert Mondavi Winery in Oakville, California *(top left, left)*, and in the Médoc region *(above)*.

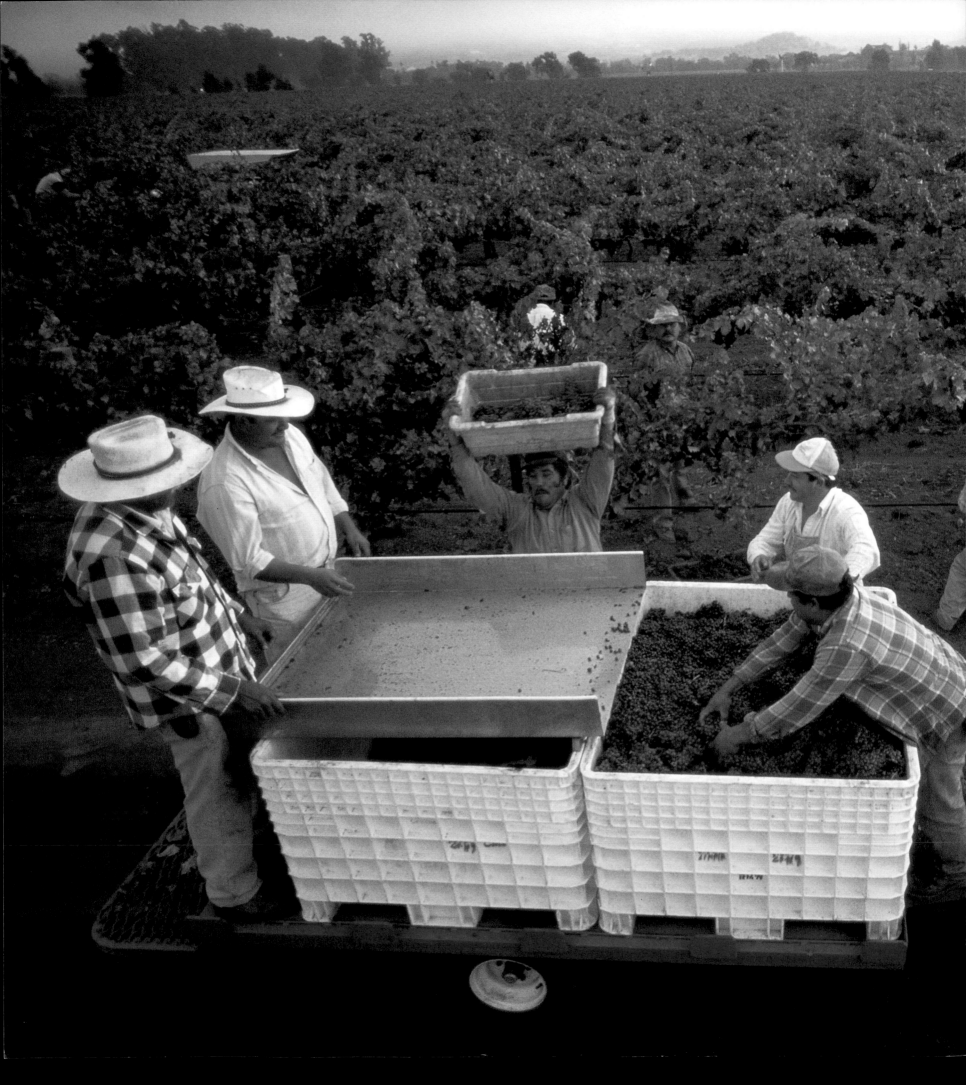

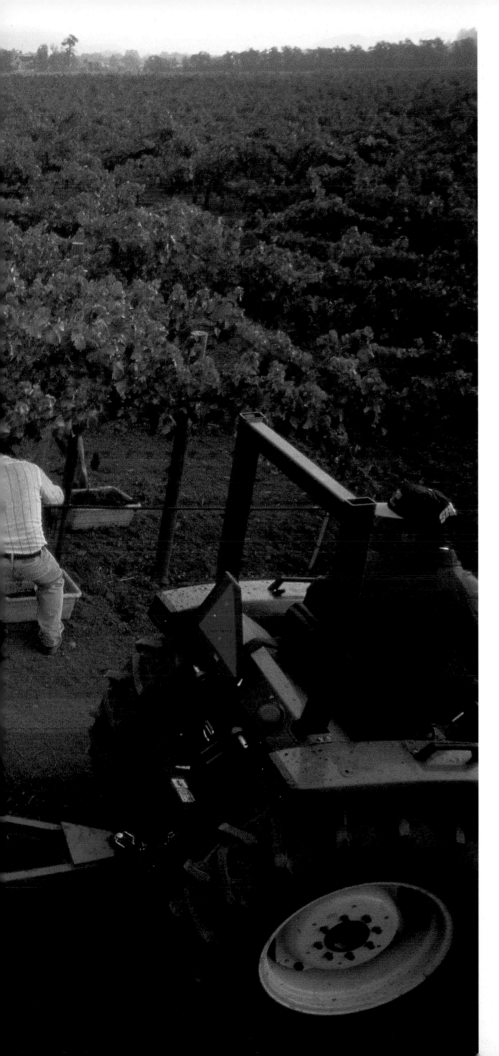

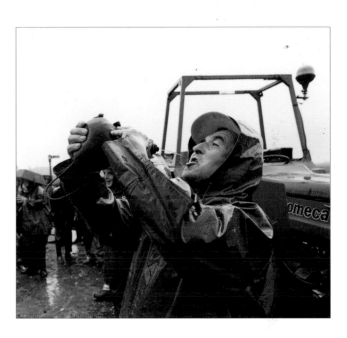

Leaves, wood, and other MOG (Materials Other than Grapes) will produce off flavors in finished wine if not removed before fermentation. A crew in a California field cleans a load of grapes before taking it to the crusher *(left)*. A migratory Spanish worker picking grapes in the Médoc region takes a break and hopes the rain will stop *(above)*. Heavy rain can cause mold contamination or can knock ripe clusters off the vines.

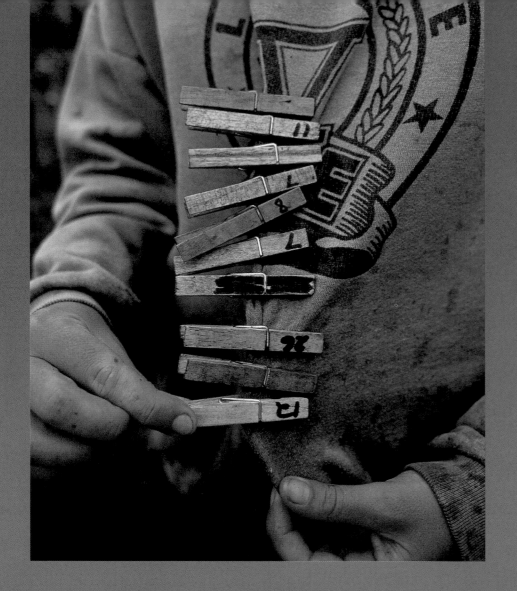

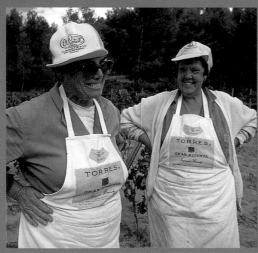

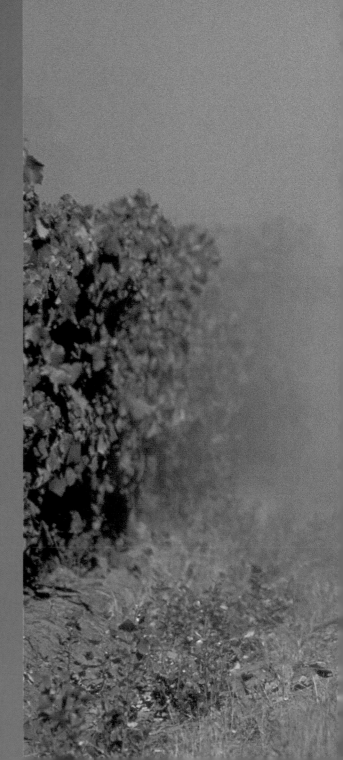

A harvest manager in the Yarra Valley of Australia uses numbered clothespins to keep track of how much each worker picks *(top)*. Spanish women pause for a break during harvest near Vilafranca del Pendès *(above)*. Happily hitching a ride on a tractor-trailer, pickers are pleased to welcome visitors to a vineyard near Curicó, Chile *(right)*.

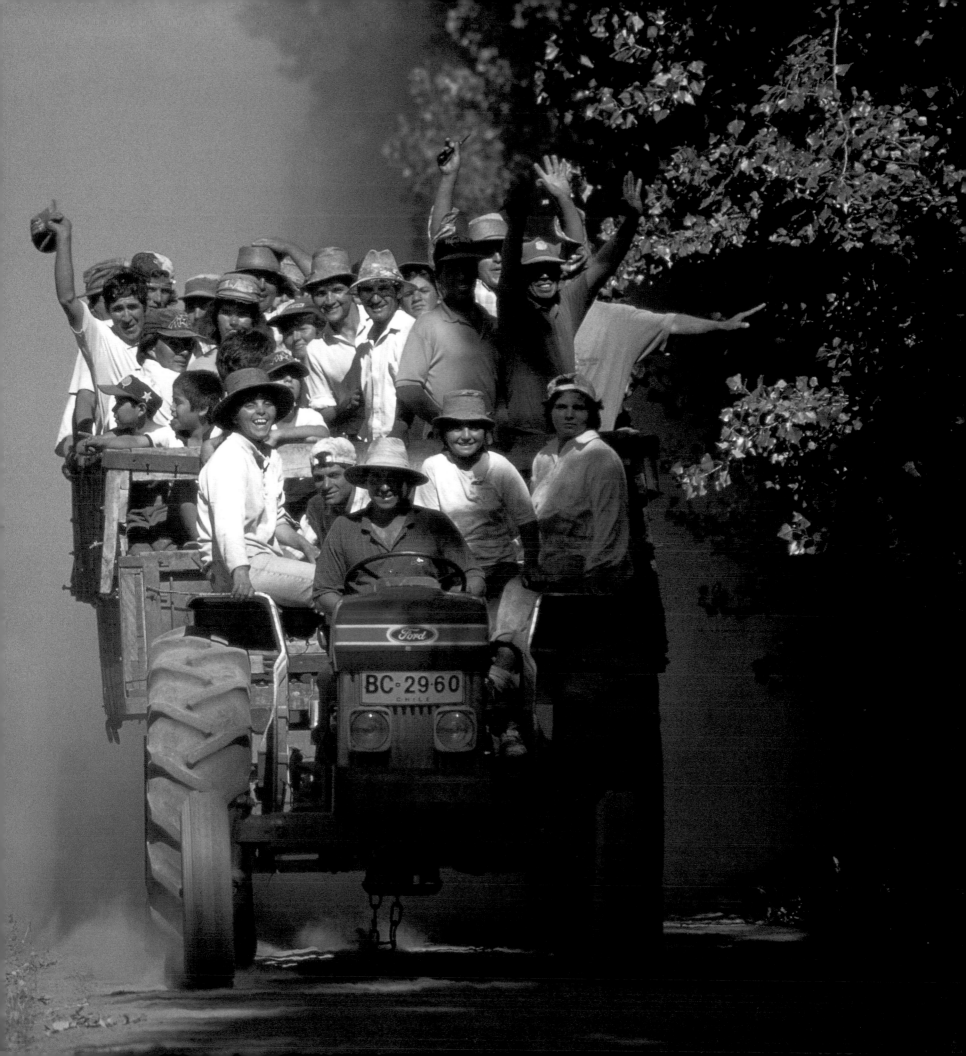

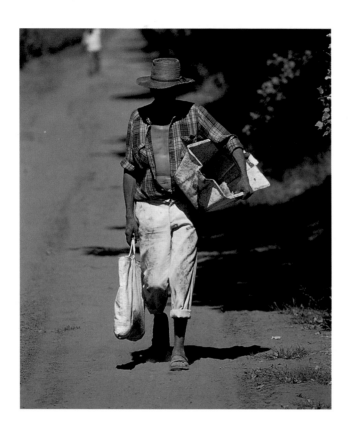

As the day ends, a vineyard worker heads home in Curicó, Chile, his pay in his pocket, his picking box feeling heavy from the weight of fatigue *(above)*. In the Médoc region, two pickers stride back to their dormitory to eat, sleep, and prepare to harvest more grapes in the morning *(right)*.

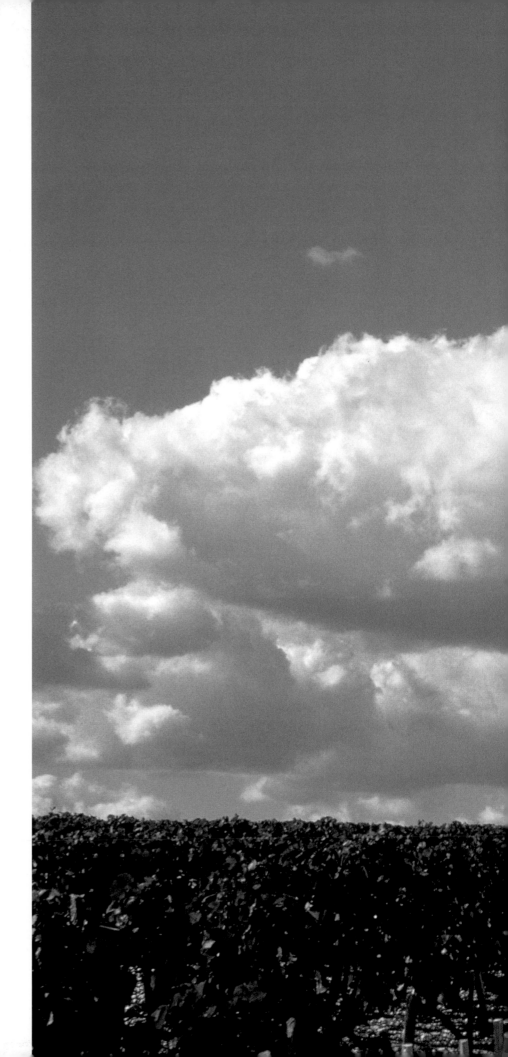

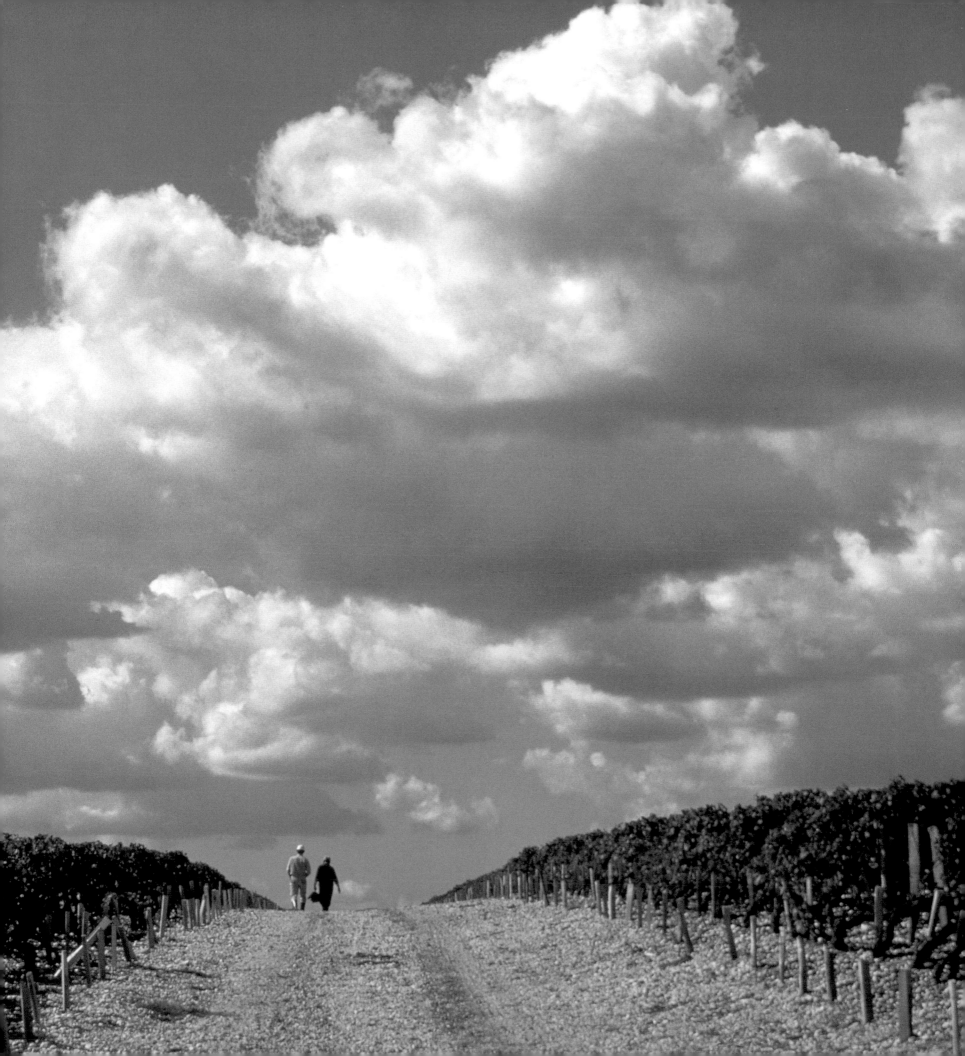

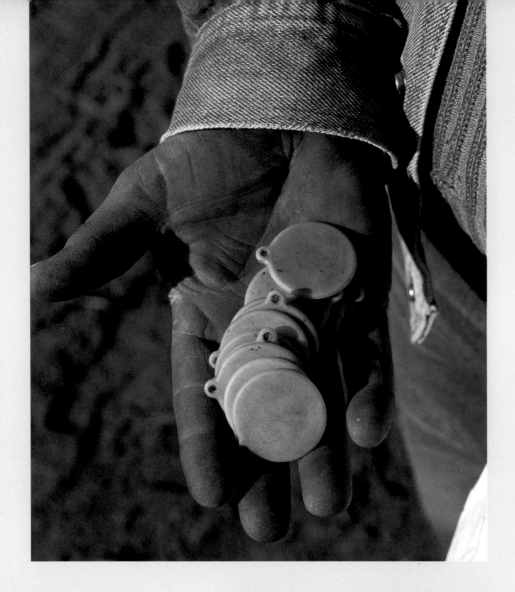

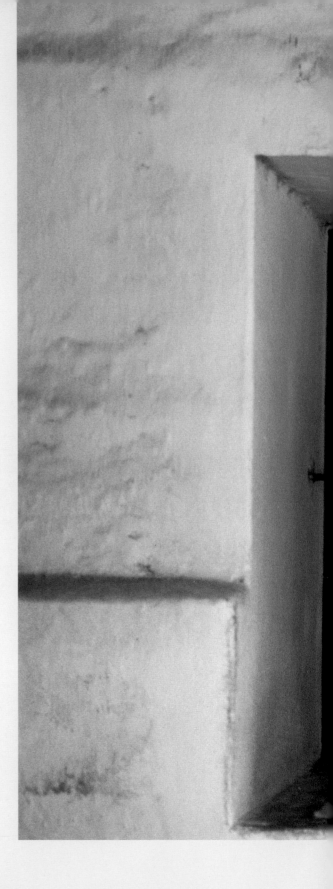

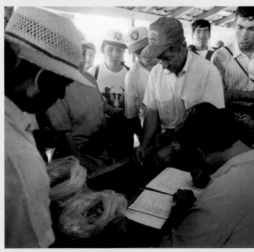

chile

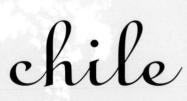

At the Caliterra winery in Chile, workers are paid according to the number of plastic chips they earn—
one chip for each basket of fruit picked *(top)*. In the same Chilean vineyard, a boss registers
each worker's production *(above)*. In addition to the daily cash payment for actual grapes picked,
workers also receive two loaves of bread from the vineyard's "Bread Office" *(right)*.

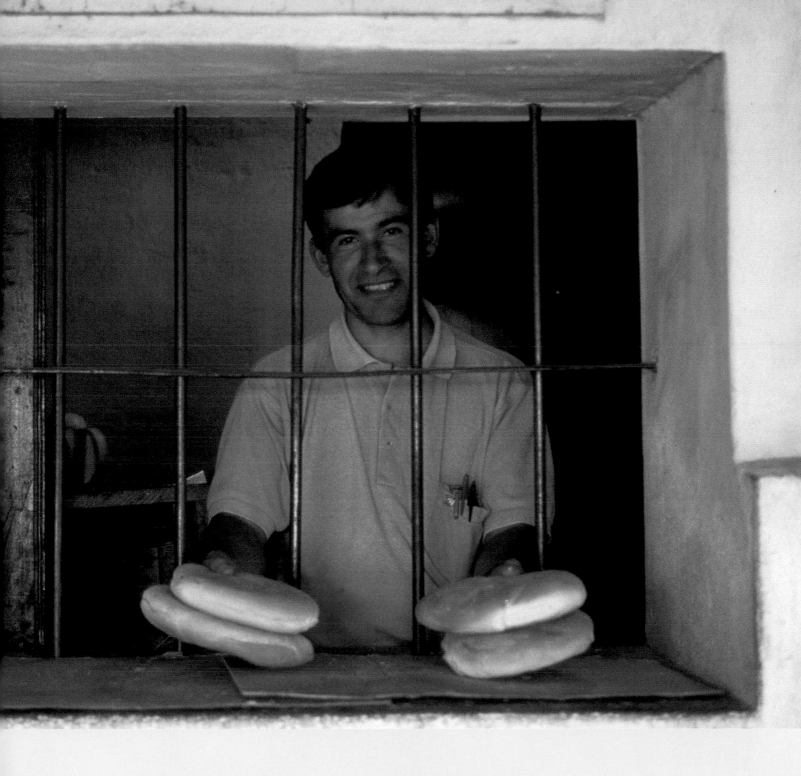

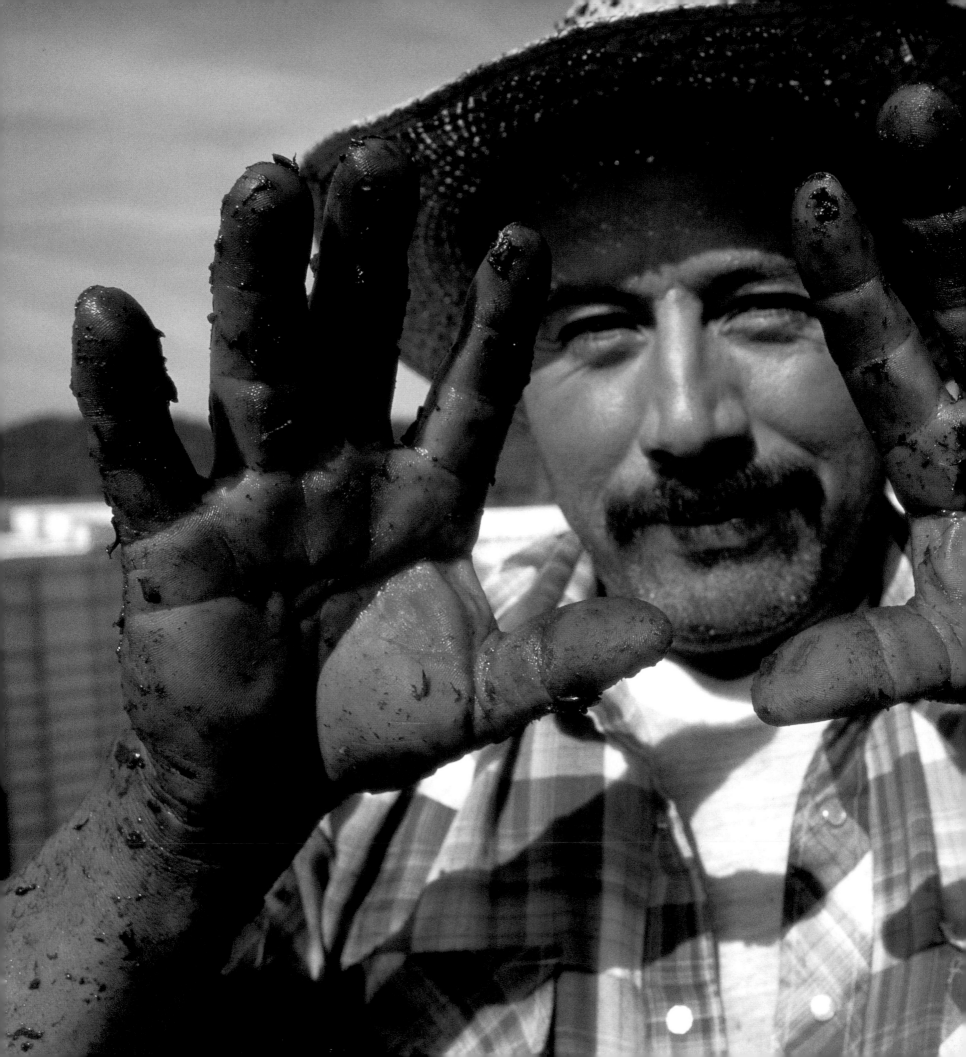

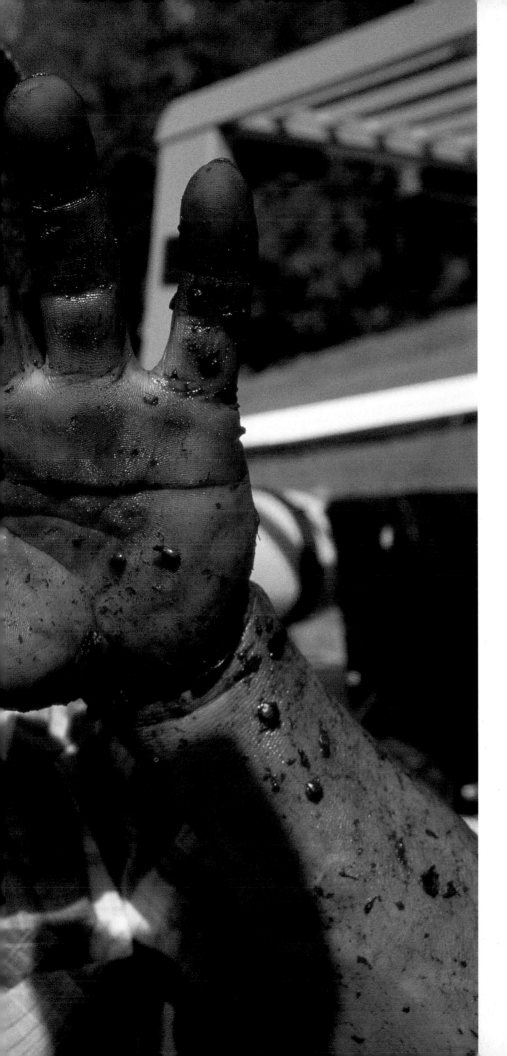

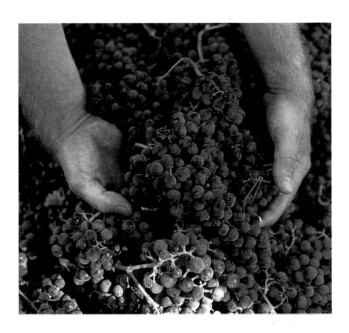

Handling cabernet grapes is a messy job, and as this worker demonstrates at Pride Mountain Vineyards in the Napa Valley, it will ruin a manicure. The intense color in the grape skins stains hands and nails with a pigment that usually doesn't fade for a week *(left)*. A handful of prime cabernet grapes at Far Niente Winery in Oakville, California, is about to be de-stemmed and crushed *(above)*. An early assessment about the quality of this new vintage will be made very soon when the winemaker samples the "must" (the mixture of juice, skins, seeds and pulp from the crusher) and measures its levels of sugar, acidity, and tannic flavor elements.

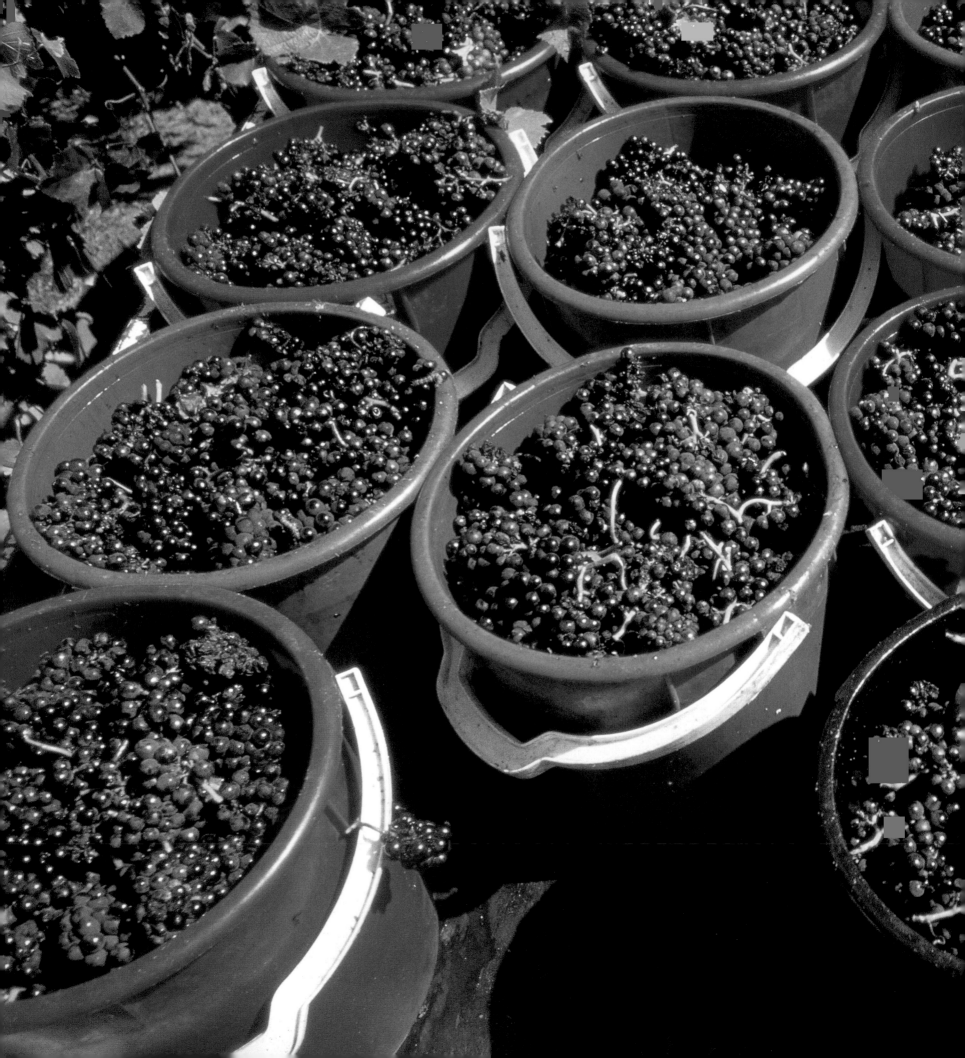

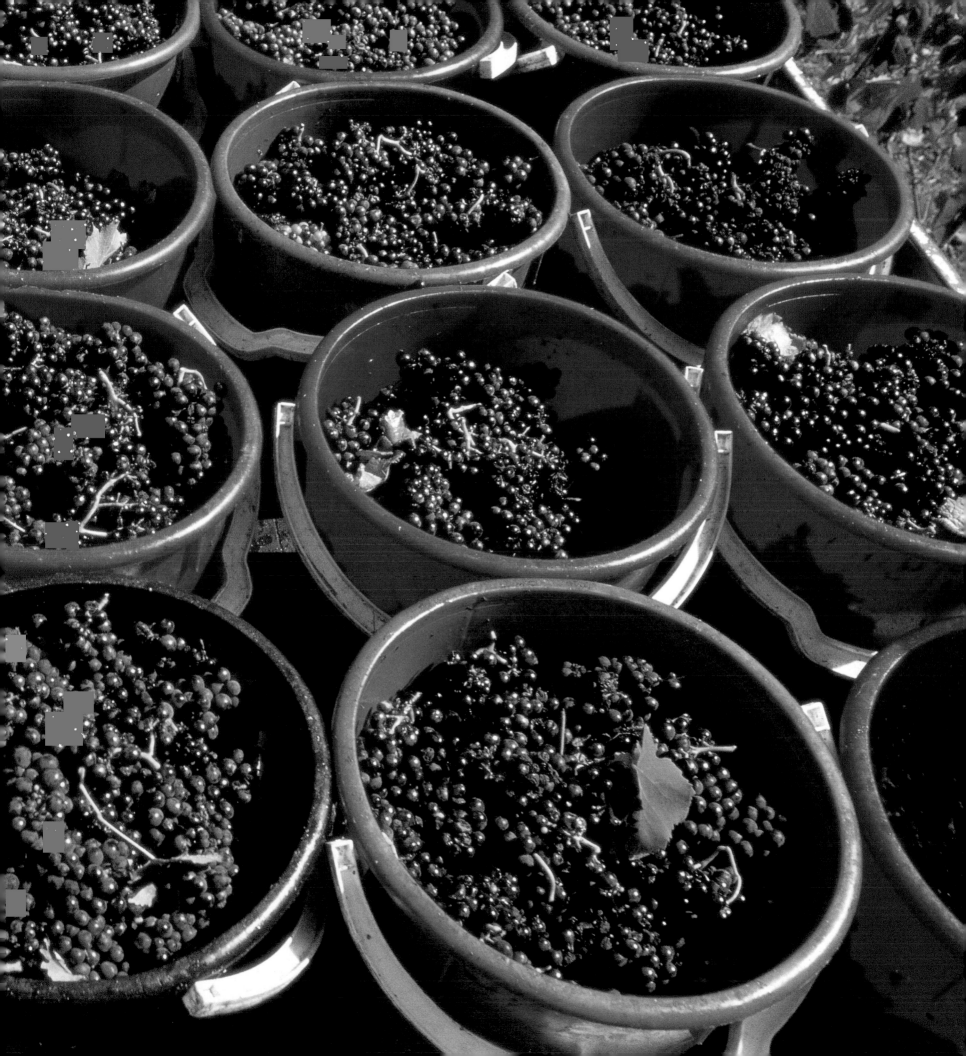

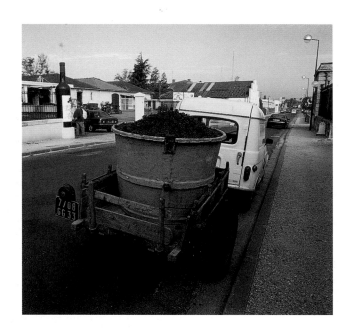

Who picked which grapes? In Australia's Coonawarra region, the answer is revealed by the different colored buckets that allow each picker to be paid precisely for the grapes he harvested *(preceding pages)*. Keeping the grapes in small buckets until taken to the crusher helps prevent oxidation of the juice, which can hamper fermentation. A farmer in Pauillac, France, hauls his harvest to the cooperative winery in which he and his neighbors share ownership *(above)*. Knee-deep in cabernet, a worker forks grapes into the crusher at Rockford Wines in the Barossa Valley of Australia *(right)*.

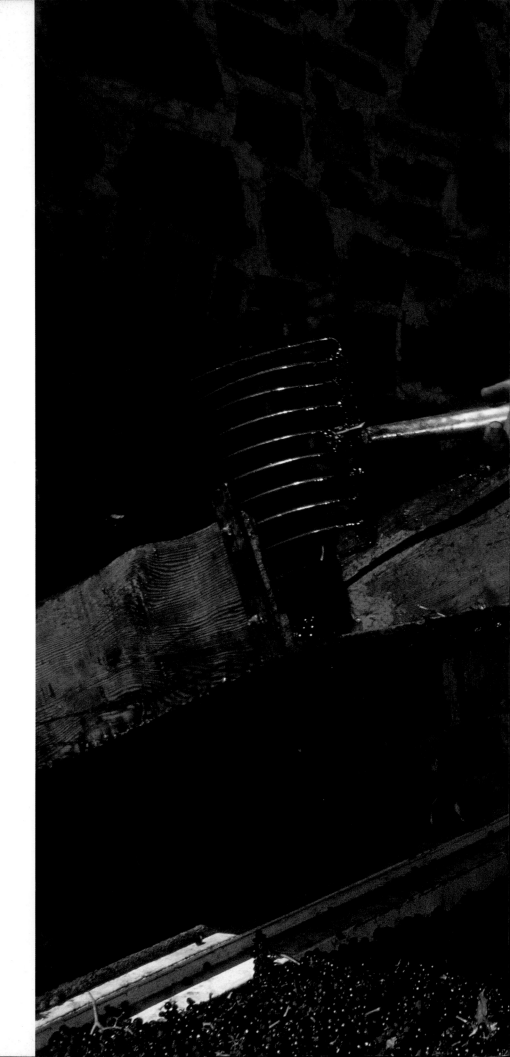

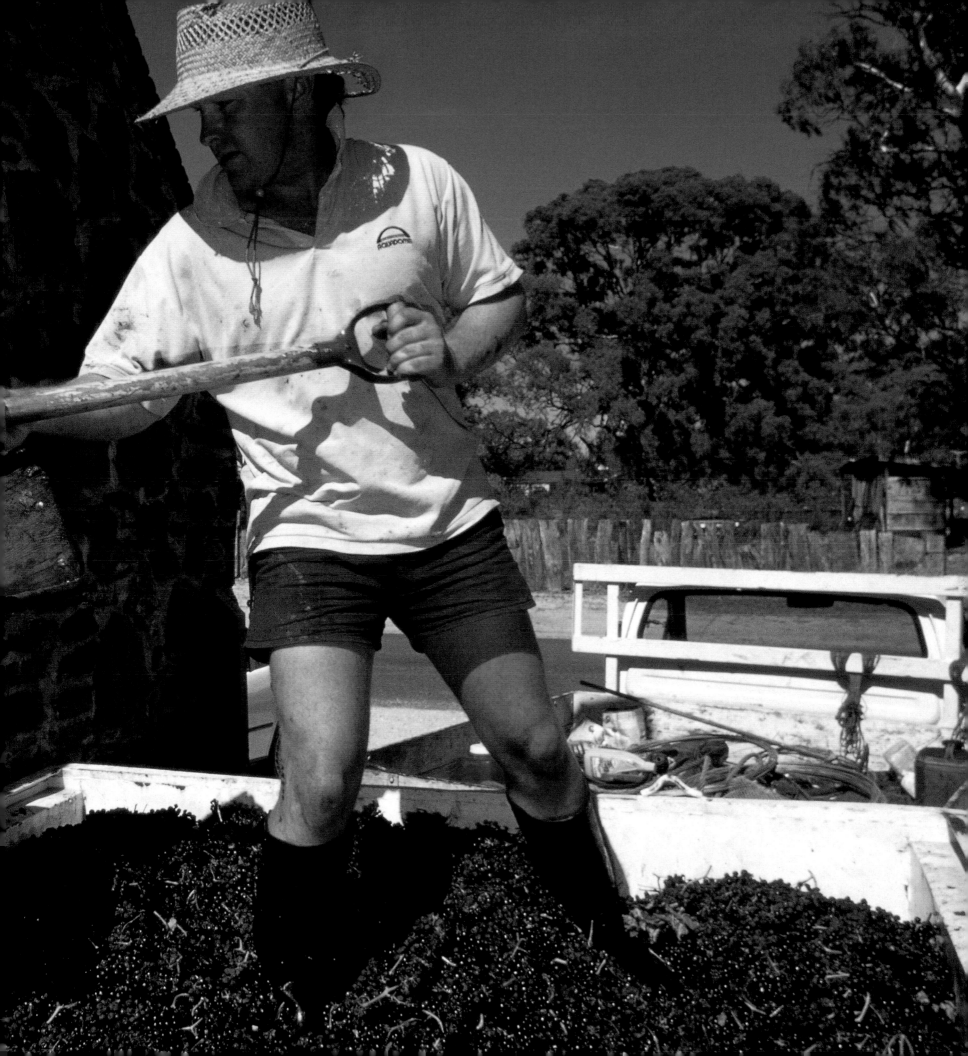

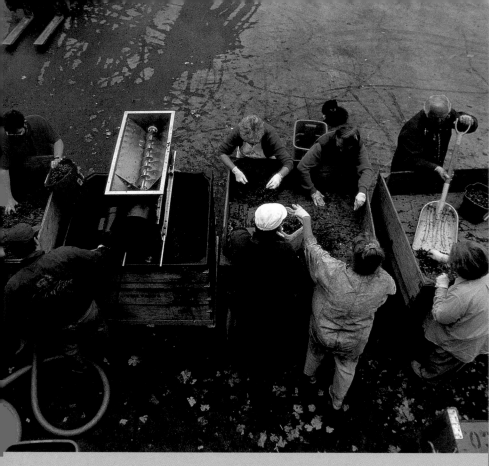

Grapes must be clean, dry, and free of damaged fruit. Care is taken by neighbors and friends to clean debris from cabernet grapes before crushing at a small winery in Woodinville, Washington *(above)*. Because the grapes are piled so deep in this bin, some of the grapes on the bottom have been crushed and begin to release free-flowing juice *(right)*. Julia Winiarski guides a bin of grapes to her family's winery crusher near Napa *(top right)*. The stems in these grape clusters will be removed by the machine before the grape berries are crushed at an Australian winery *(far right)*.

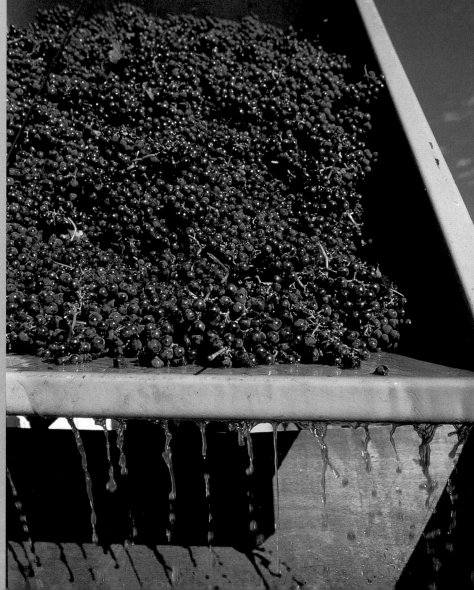

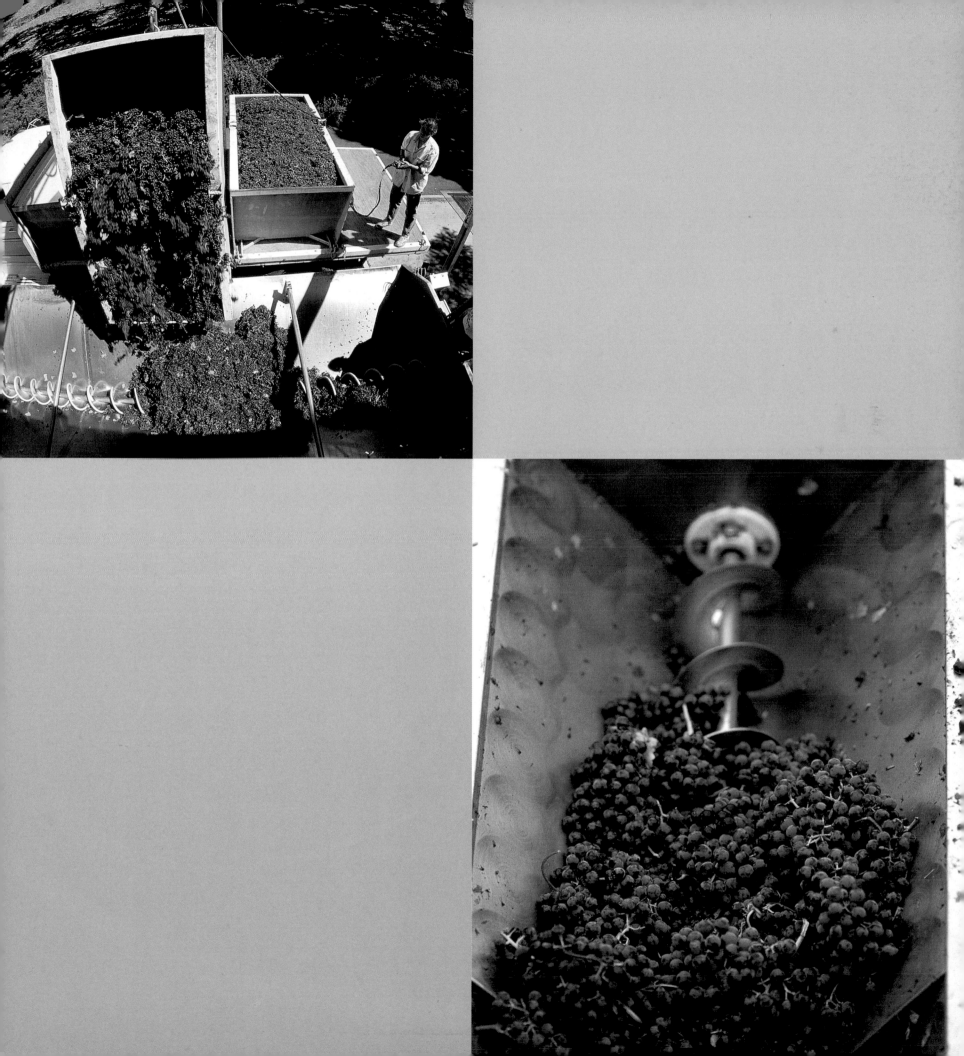

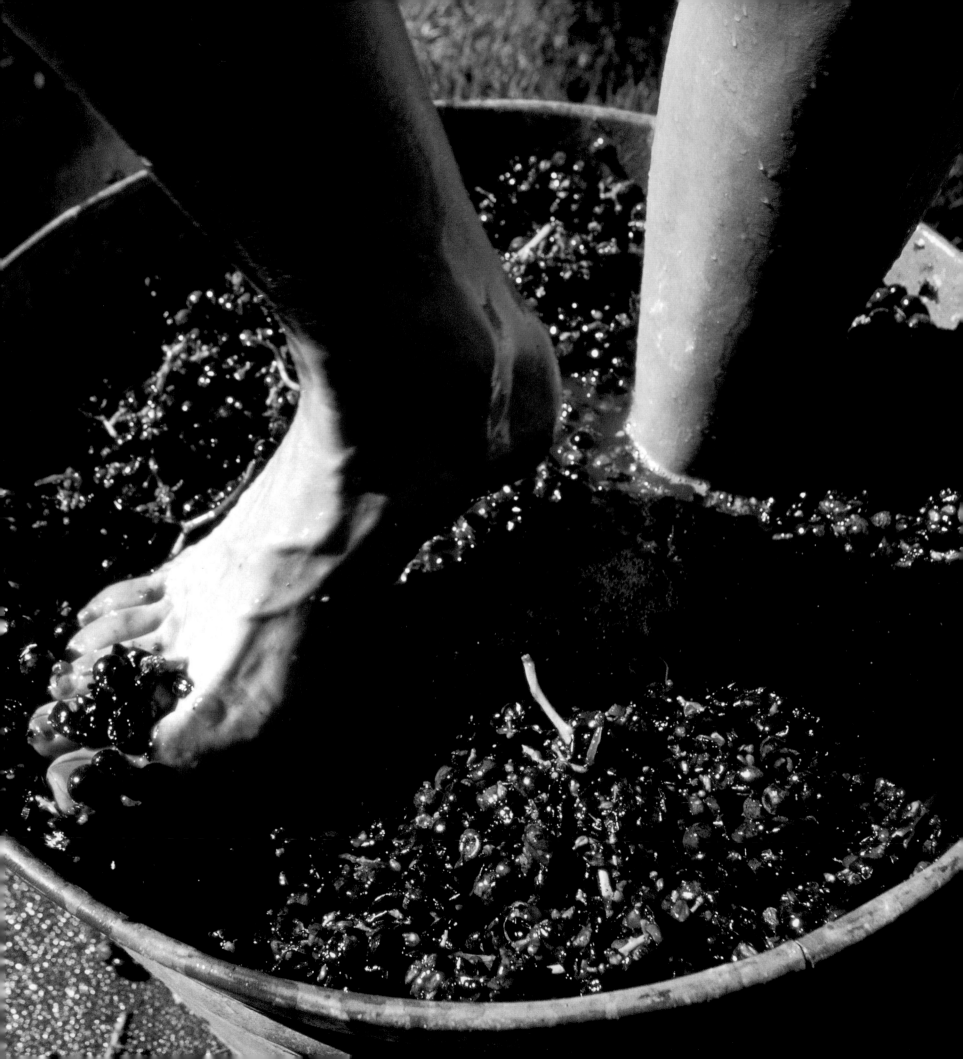

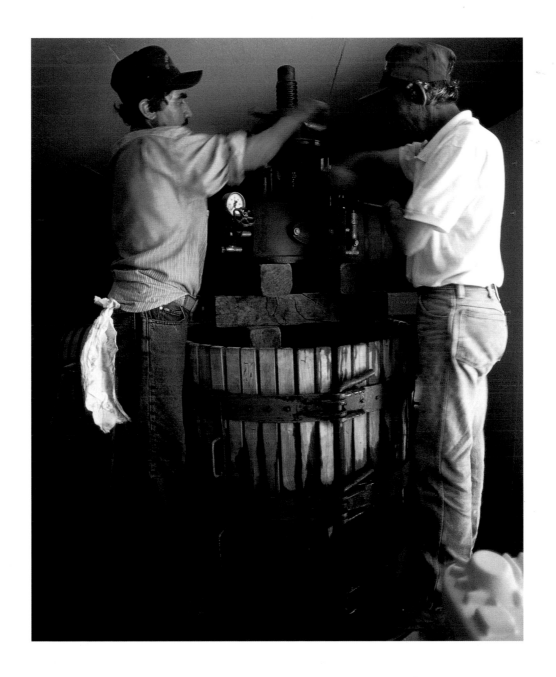

A home winemaker attempts to keep tradition alive with a session of
cabernet stomping. The job is done when all the berries have been split and the skins are floating
on top *(left)*. After fermentation, the new wine is separated from the skins and seeds.
This basket press at Long Vineyards in St. Helena, California, squeezes out the last 10 percent of
this year's new wine from the residue left in the fermentation vat *(above)*.

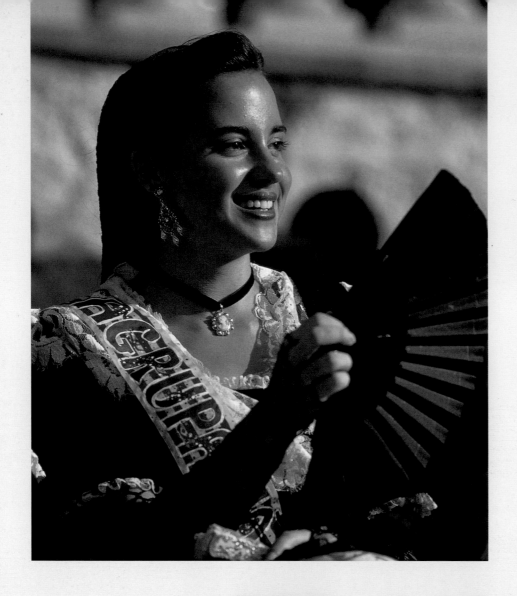

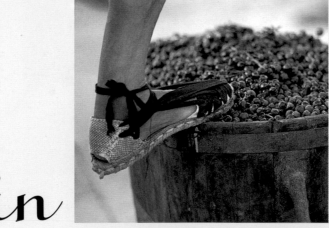

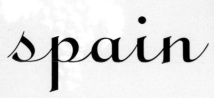

spain

The harvest is festival time in Spain as thousands of visitors flock to

the town of Sitges. Early in the day, a candidate for festival queen charms the judges *(top)*.

Later, an eager contestant is poised to begin the grape-stomping competition *(above)*.

Only special guests are invited to view the traditional dances performed at the Miguel Torres Winery *(right)*.

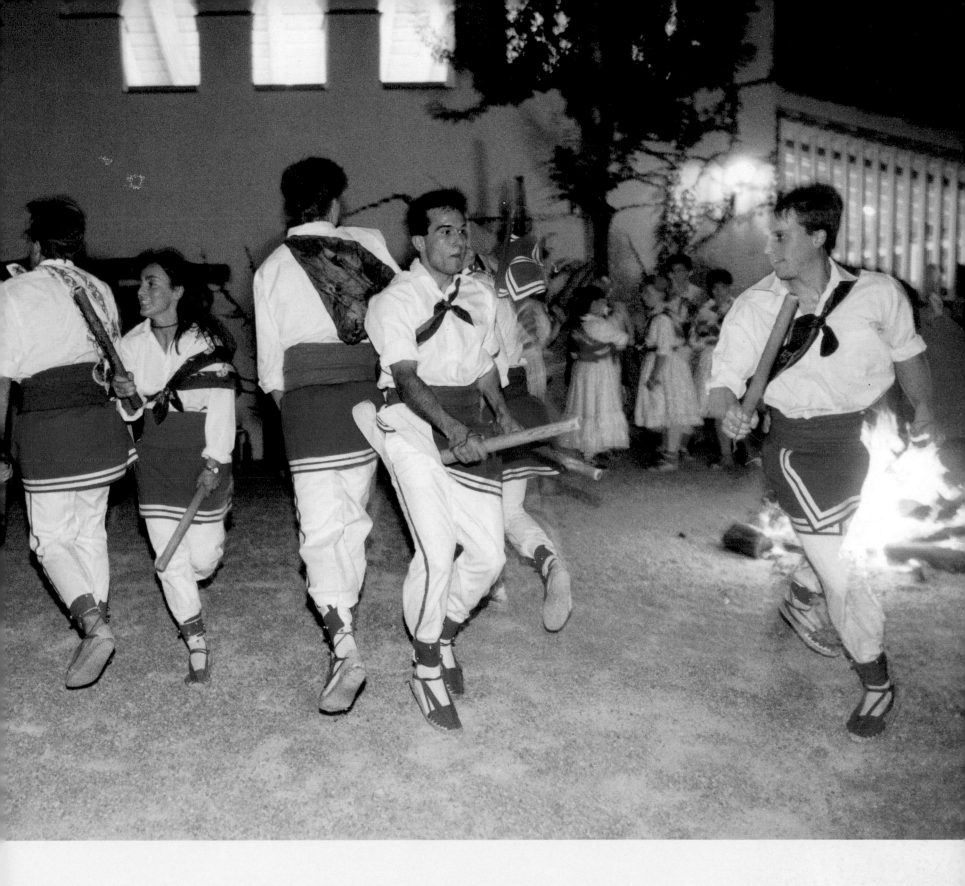

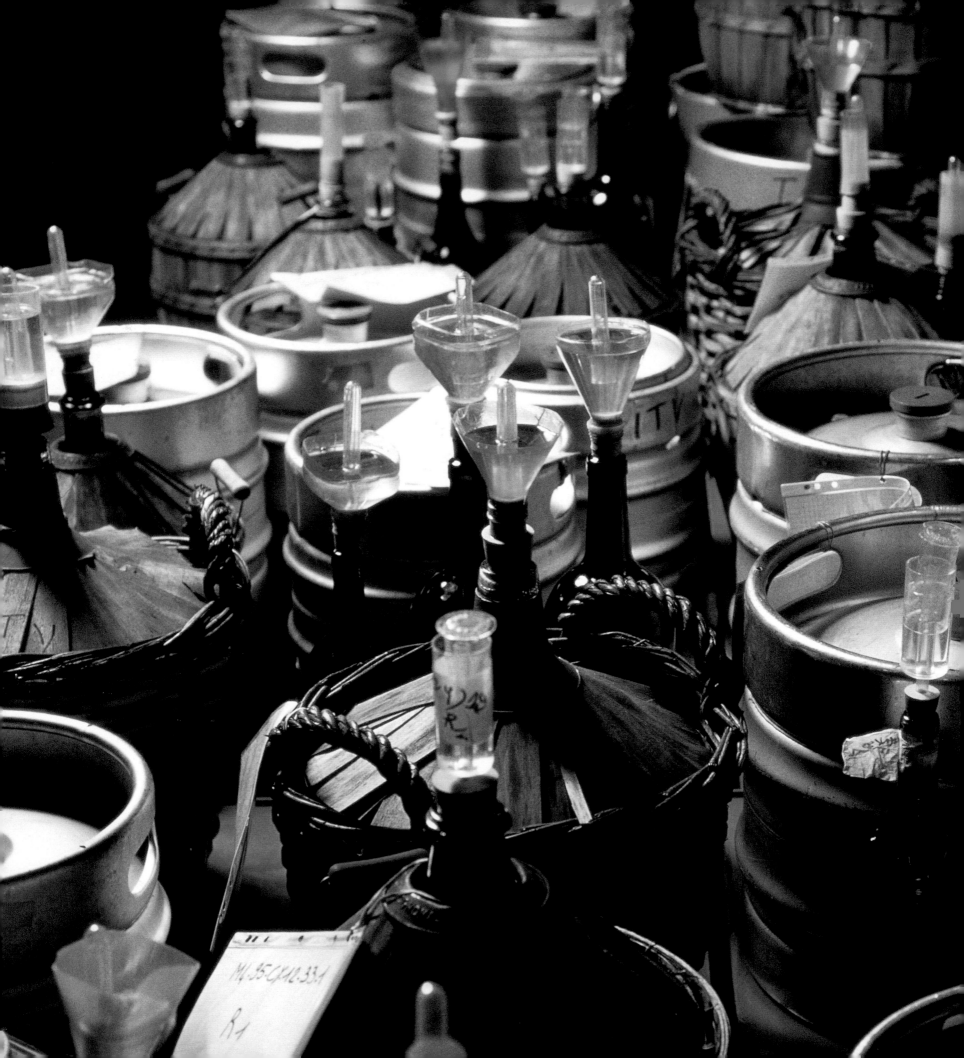

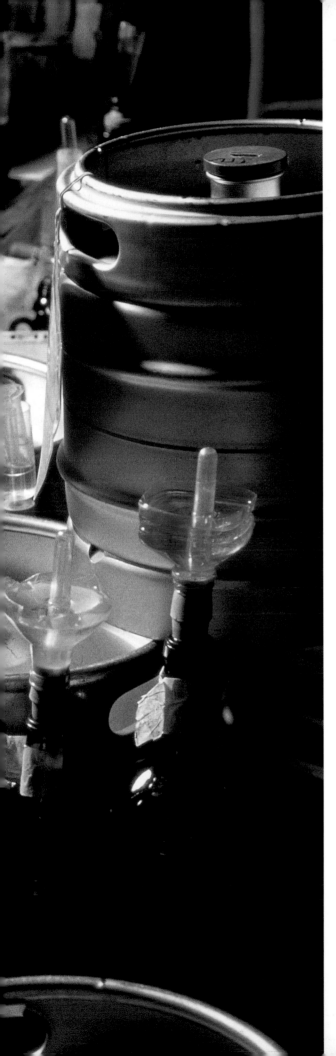

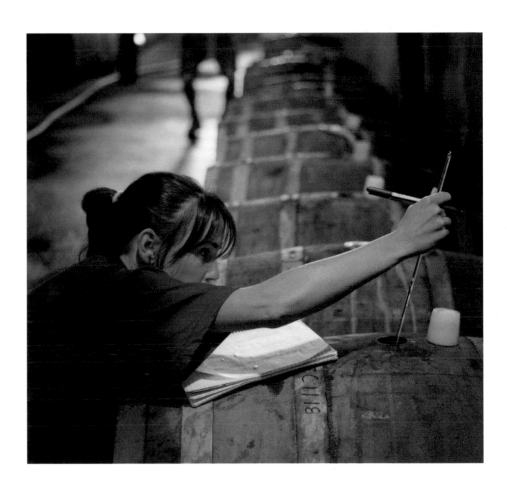

Wine fermentation normally takes place when the "must" is kept between 80 and 95 degrees Fahrenheit. Too hot will kill the yeast, too cold will put it to sleep. A technician checks the temperature of the unfinished wine in Chile *(above)*. Even after two centuries of making the world's finest wines, enologists in Bordeaux continue to search for improvements. At Chambre d'Agriculture de la Gironde in Blanquefort, France, they experiment with microfermentation and aging processes *(left)*. *The Grapecrusher*, a statue by Gino Miles, welcomes visitors to Napa Valley *(following page)*.

"Cabernet can show exquisite finesse and elegance, with the most

LEN EVANS, O.B.E.
POKOLBIN, AUSTRALIA

delicious complex flavors—

incredibly intense, yet light

and subtle."

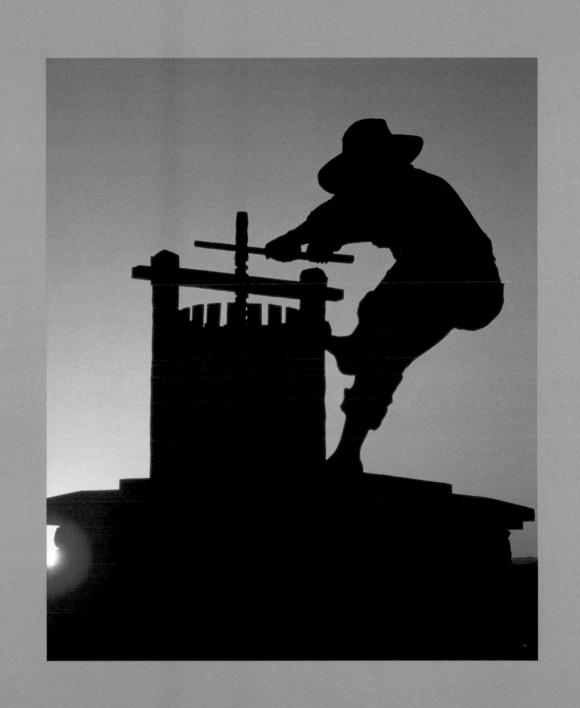

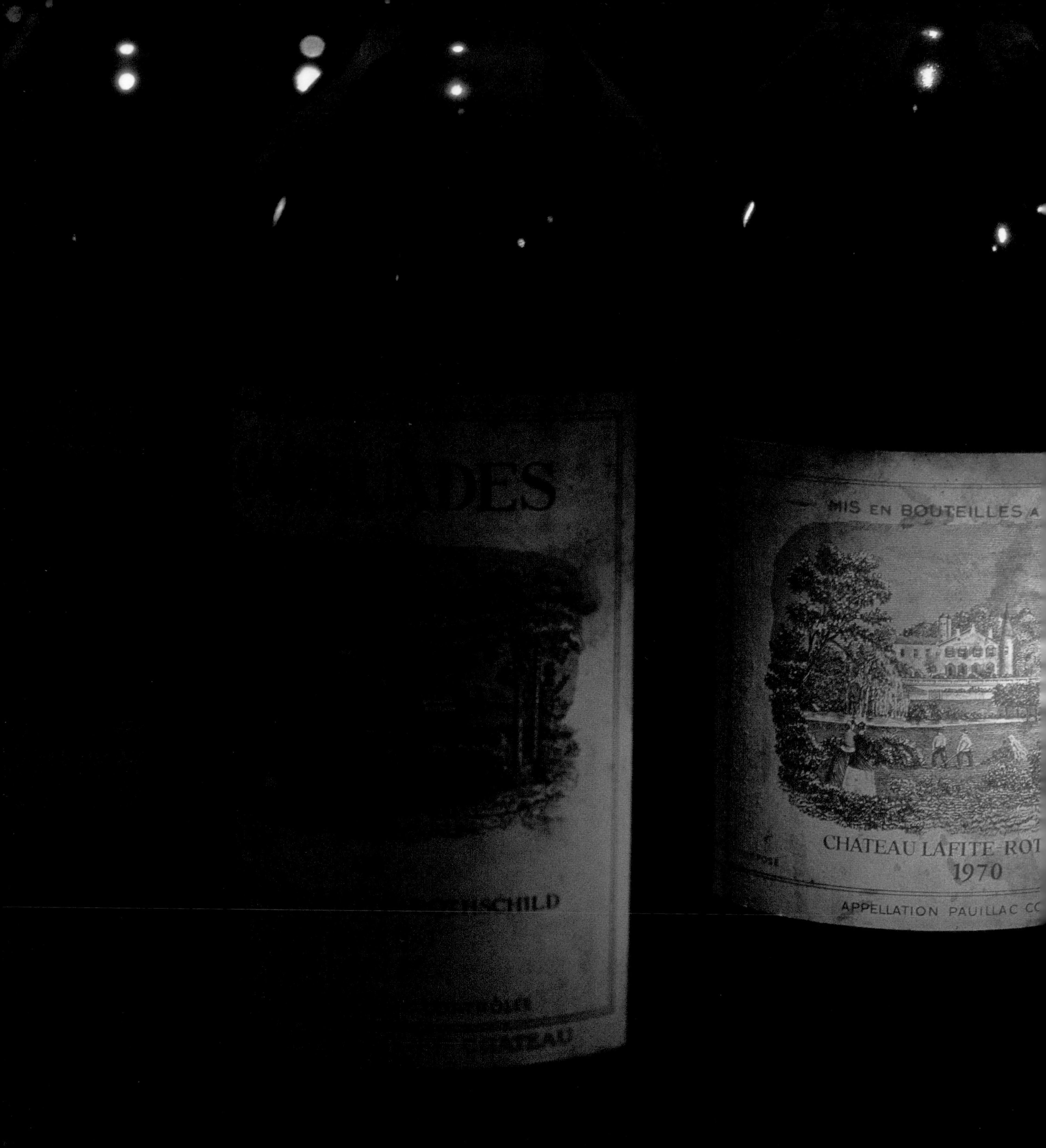

...DES

MIS EN BOUTEILLES A

CHATEAU LAFITE-ROT
1970

...SCHILD

APPELLATION PAUILLAC CC

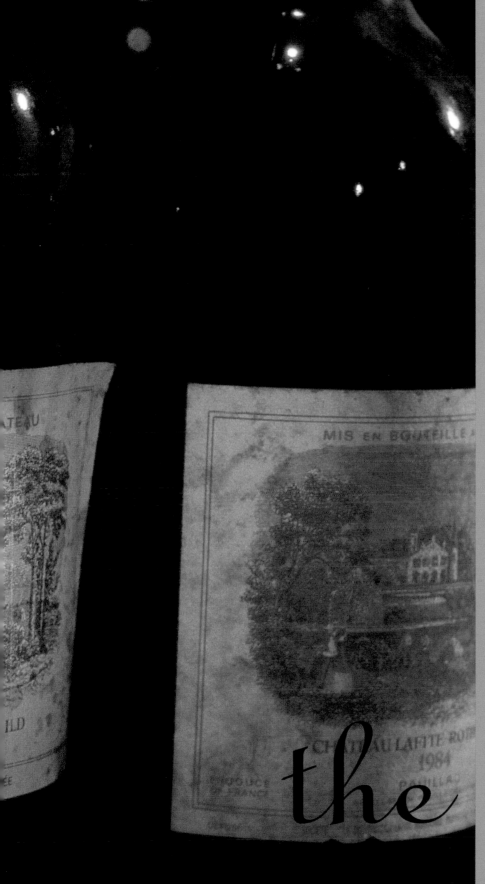

chapter four
CABERNET

the wine

Following its frenzied birth during the harvest, the young Cabernet, direct from the fermentation vat, is typically undrinkably harsh, with a strong and generally abrasive personality. In order to achieve the aristocratic elegance for which Cabernet is celebrated, it must endure several years of quiet discipline in the aging cellar.

Red wines need aging because they contain compounds that continue to undergo a slow conversion and must be gently removed. That's especially true of Cabernet Sauvignon, which is blessed with an abundance of phenolics that provide color, aroma, and flavor.

Aging is a complex process that demands careful attention. Critical questions must be considered that will determine exactly what kind of aging, storing, and blending will be required to shape the raw wine into the character of a fine Cabernet Sauvignon. Will the wine from one vineyard be blended with the product of other grapes? Will it be stored in new barrels that impart a strong wood flavor or in barrels that have been used before? How long will the wine stay in the barrels?

These judgments are made by experienced winemakers who taste, blend, and guide the young wines toward maturity. Just as a thoroughbred isn't a racehorse until it has been trained, Cabernet Sauvignon doesn't achieve its potential until it has been carefully aged.

Within two or three years, the harsh raw wine that flowed from the fermenter has grown up and become smooth enough to be suited up in glass. It's ready for bottling.

But even after bottling, Cabernet Sauvignon still has some aging to do. Now, in a cork-sealed, but not absolutely airtight bottle, different kinds of transformations take place. The aggressive flavors soften and aromas evolve into what is called the "bouquet." Depth and complexity are revealed, and years after they were harvested in the vineyard, the cabernet grapes have been transformed into a fine wine.

For all the science that has been developed to track the process, and despite the volumes of research done to guarantee good wine every time, creating a great Cabernet Sauvignon is still very much an art.

Perhaps that need for human judgment is what makes wine so popular. In a world that relies ever more on technology to make our key decisions there is something natural, romantic, and comfortable about wine. There's an intimacy in sharing the contents of the same bottle with other humans that helps us link our spirits and not just our minds.

But in the end, perhaps the most important reason we care about wine, especially Cabernet Sauvignon, is that after we've carefully illustrated the art, annotated all the science, and examined the ritual of making wine, the real story of how it's created and why we feel so drawn to it is still a mystery.

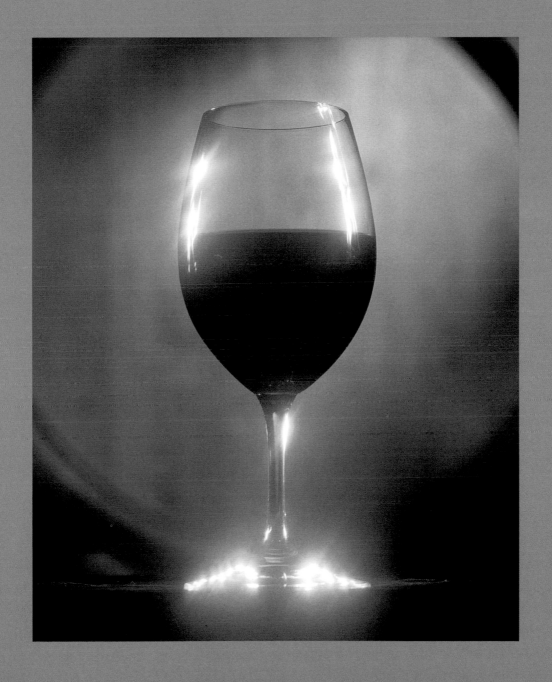

Proud labels on old bottles recall the excellence of past vintages at a wine shop
in Pauillac, France *(preceding pages)*. The opacity that distinguishes Cabernet Sauvignon
from other wines is unmistakable in this formal portrait *(above)*.

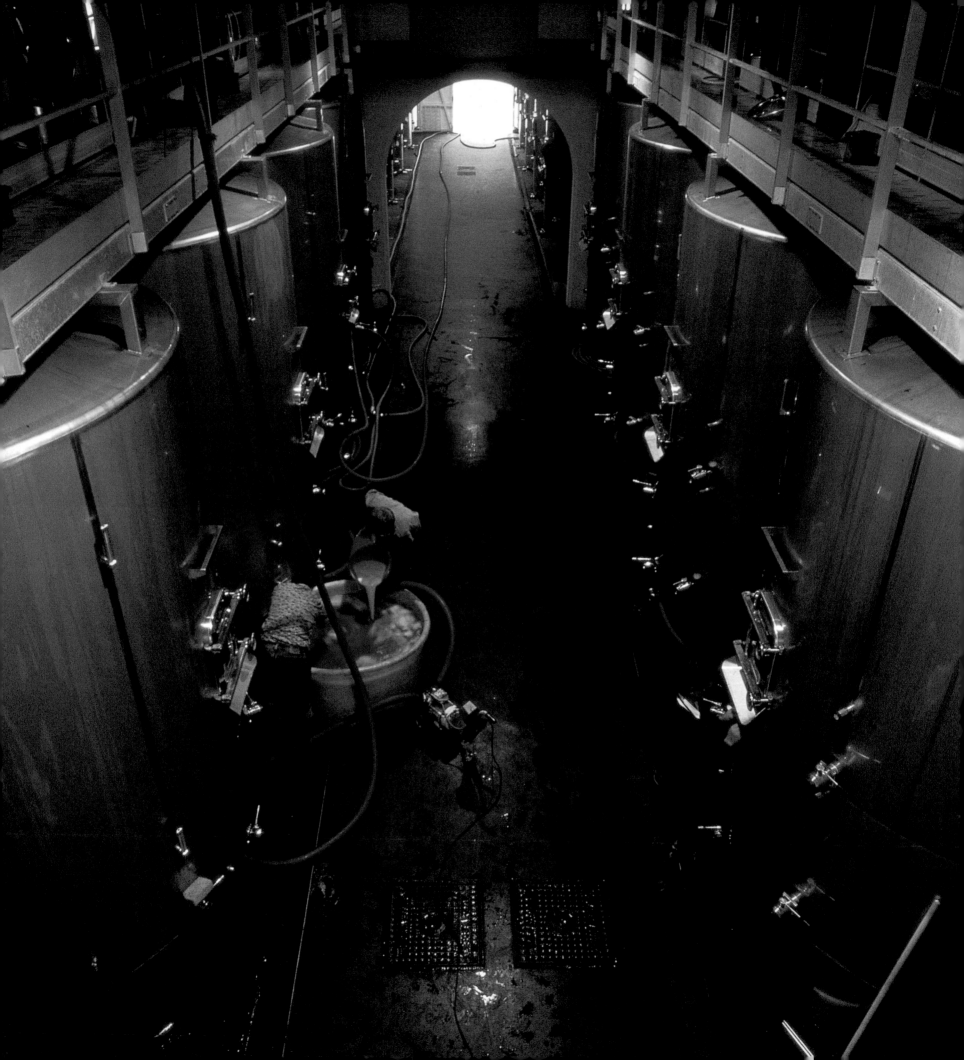

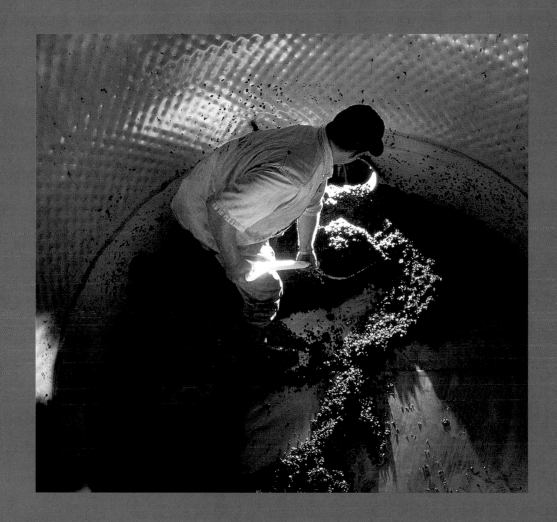

Unfinished wine glows red as it is pumped from the bottom of a stainless steel tank in
France and is returned to the top of the skins and pulp of the "must" *(left)*. This step is important
because red wine acquires its intense coloring and flavors from contact with the skins during
the fermenting process. Shoveling pomace, or grape debris from a fermenter, is only one step in
the handwork required in winemaking *(above)*. Wine pressed from the pomace has a stronger
taste than the free-run wine from these same grapes.

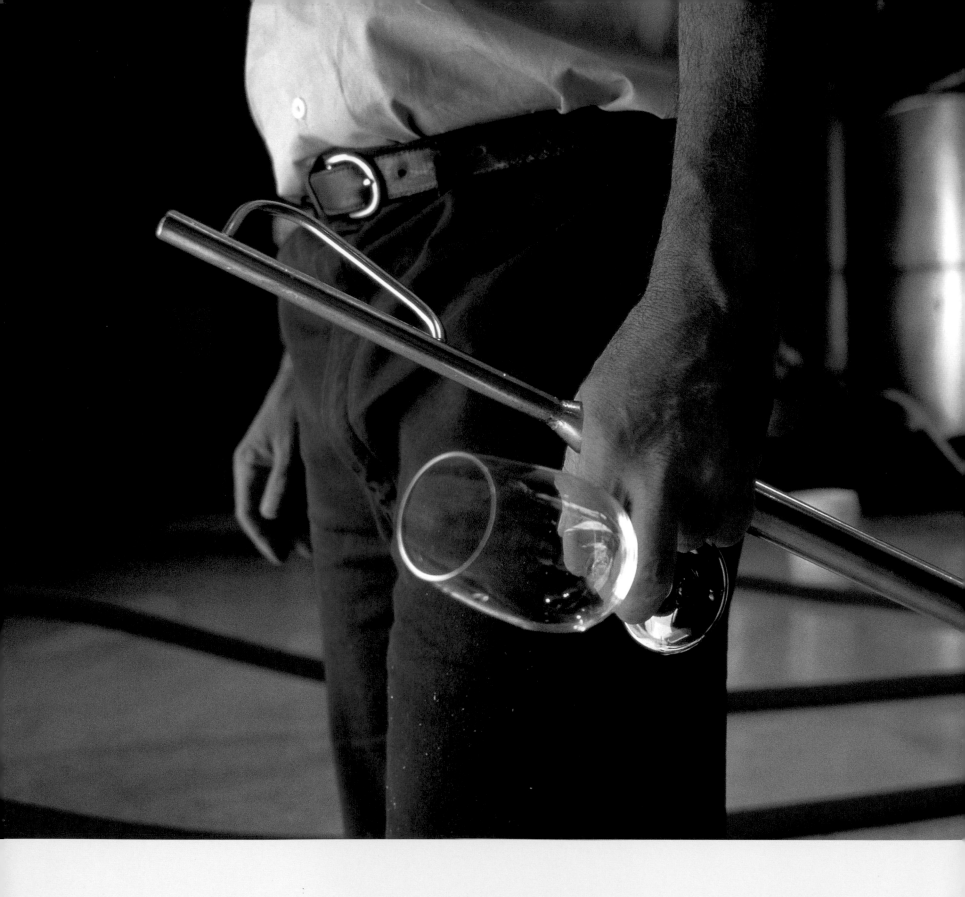

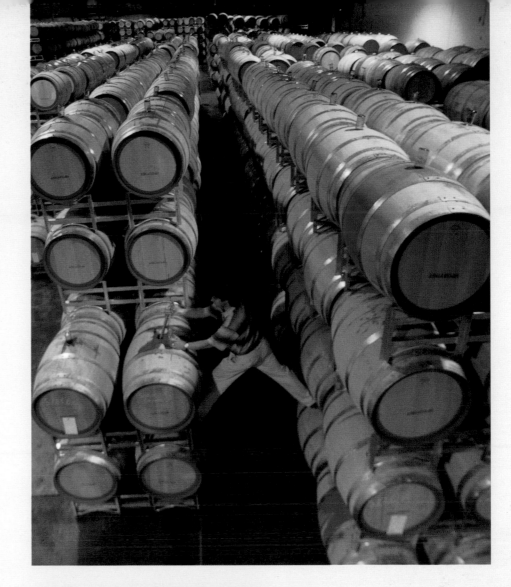

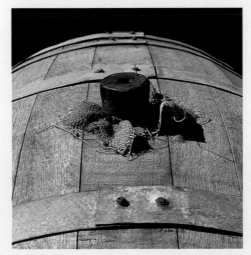

australia

On the way to sample wine at Peter Lehmann Wines in Australia, a winemaker carries a "thief," which suctions small quantities from the barrel. The sample will help determine how long to keep the Cabernet in barrels, whether another process will be required to remove fine particles and improve clarity, and whether the temperature in some of the barrels should be changed to promote a different reaction *(left)*.

At Penfolds in the Barossa Valley, it's a stretch to reach barrels *(top)*. Burlap holds a "bung" in place at another Barossa Valley winery *(above)*.

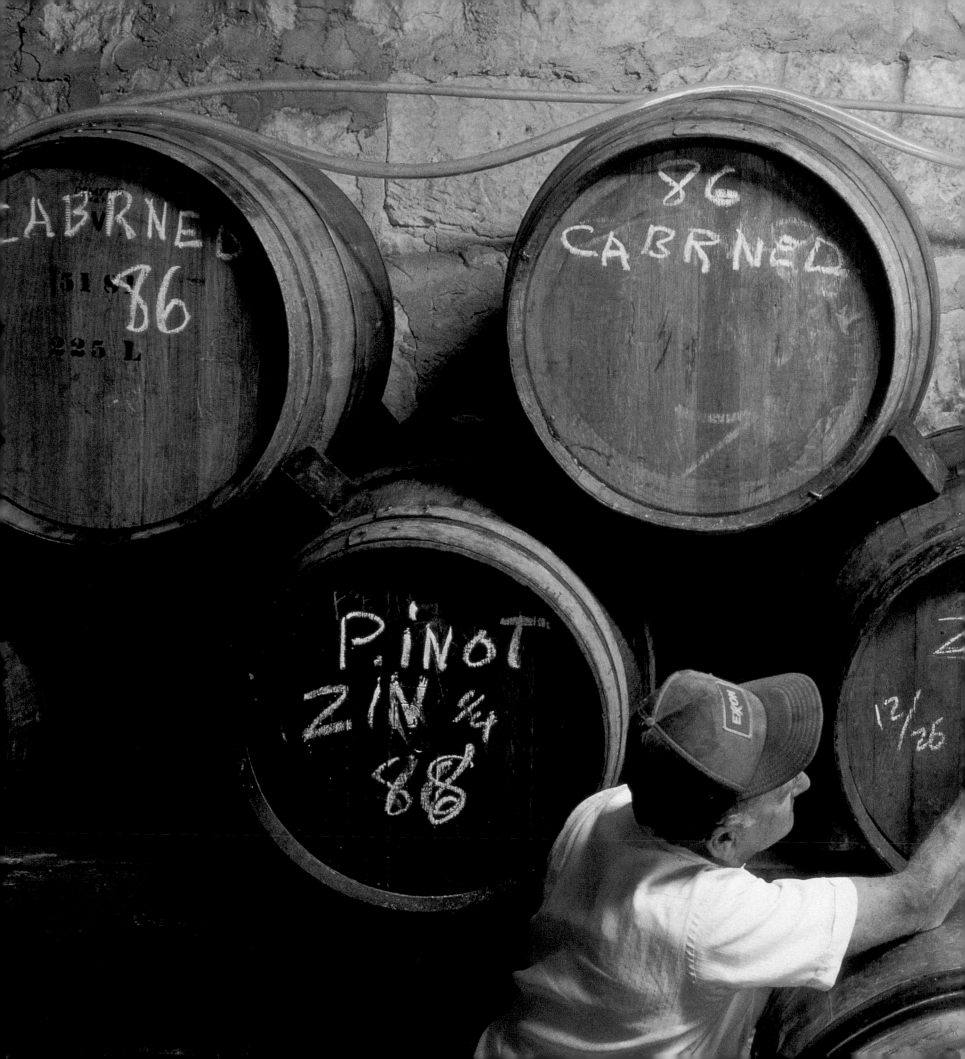

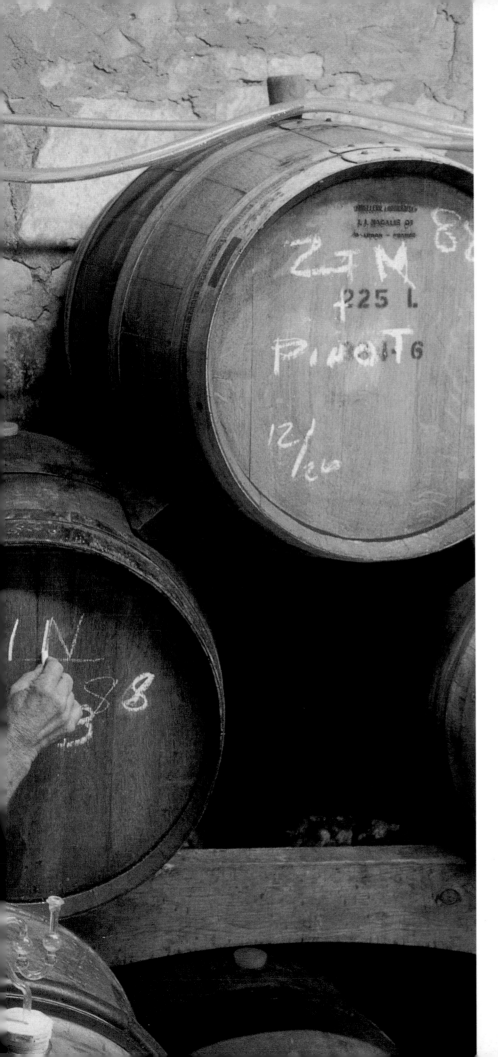

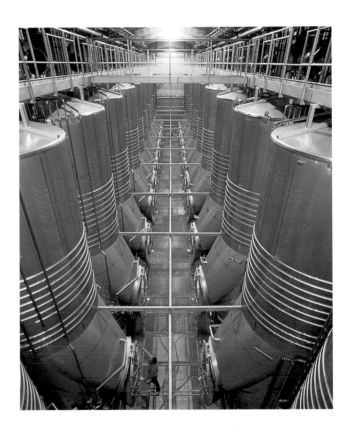

Carefully identifying the wine in each barrel is just
as important for Angelo Regusci's private winery in the Napa
Valley *(left)*, as it is in this ultramodern cooperative winery
near Bordeaux *(above)* where 300 local growers bring grapes
from their vineyards. In an effort to obtain higher yields
while maintaining quality, many vintners are choosing stainless
steel tanks such as these over traditional wooden barrels.

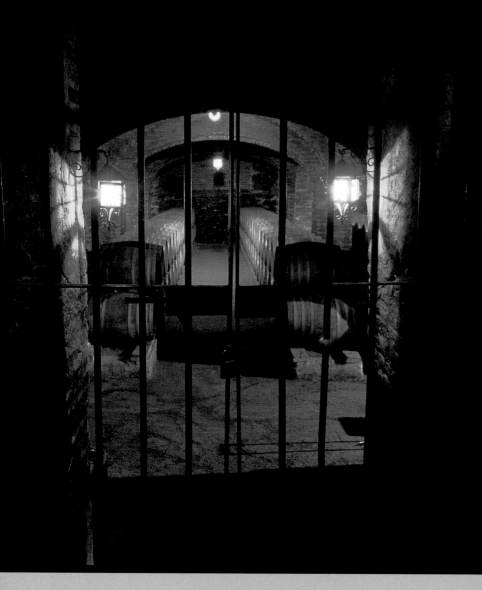

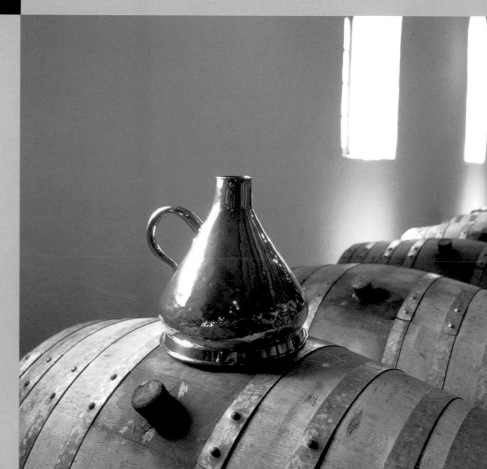

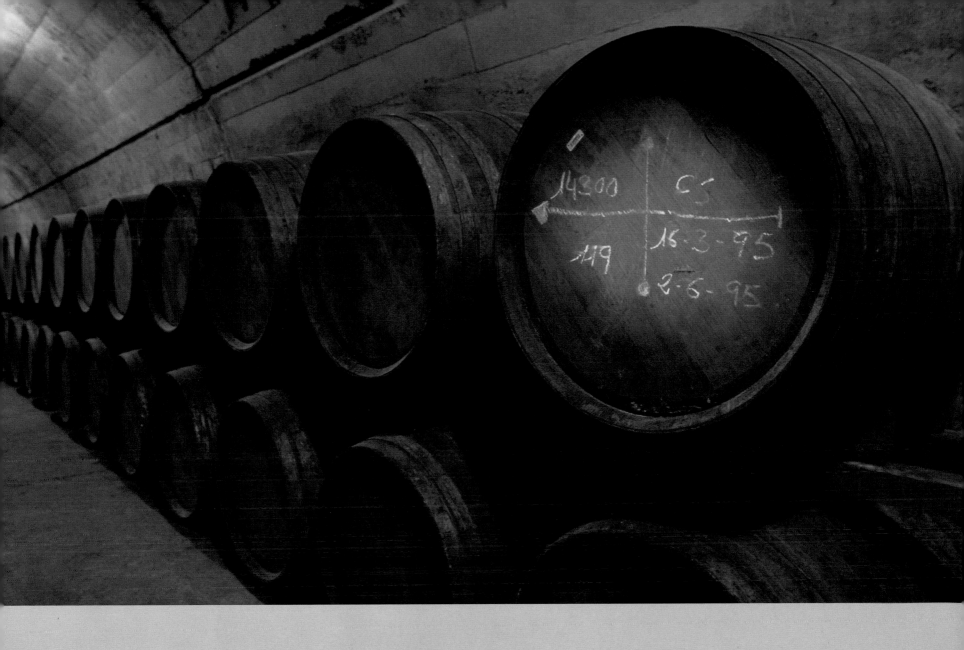

Making fine red wines requires care not just in the growing and harvesting of outstanding grapes, but in the final aging and bottling processes as well. In the century-old cave of Viña Santa Rita near Santiago, Chile, metal gates symbolize the vintner's responsibility to safeguard and improve the young wine entrusted to the aging cellars *(top left)*. At L'Ormarins Estate, founded in 1694, in the Franschhoek Valley of South Africa, copper funnels are for decoration only; the copper could affect the flavor of the wine *(left)*. The temperature of the 6,000 barrels in Cava Josefa at Miguel Torres near Barcelona, Spain, is very close to the ideal constant of 58 degrees Fahrenheit *(above)*. The bulk of the wine aging in barrels at Opus One Winery in Oakville, California, is Cabernet Sauvignon *(following pages)*.

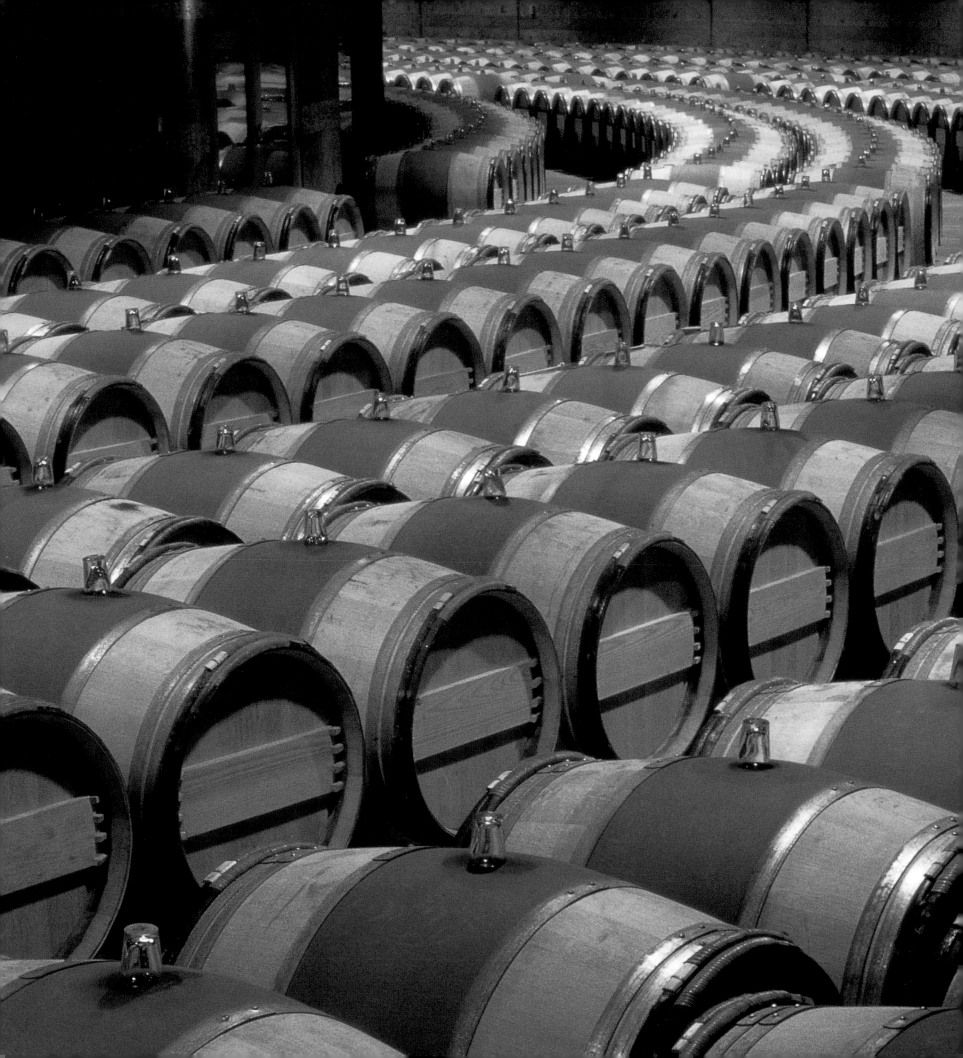

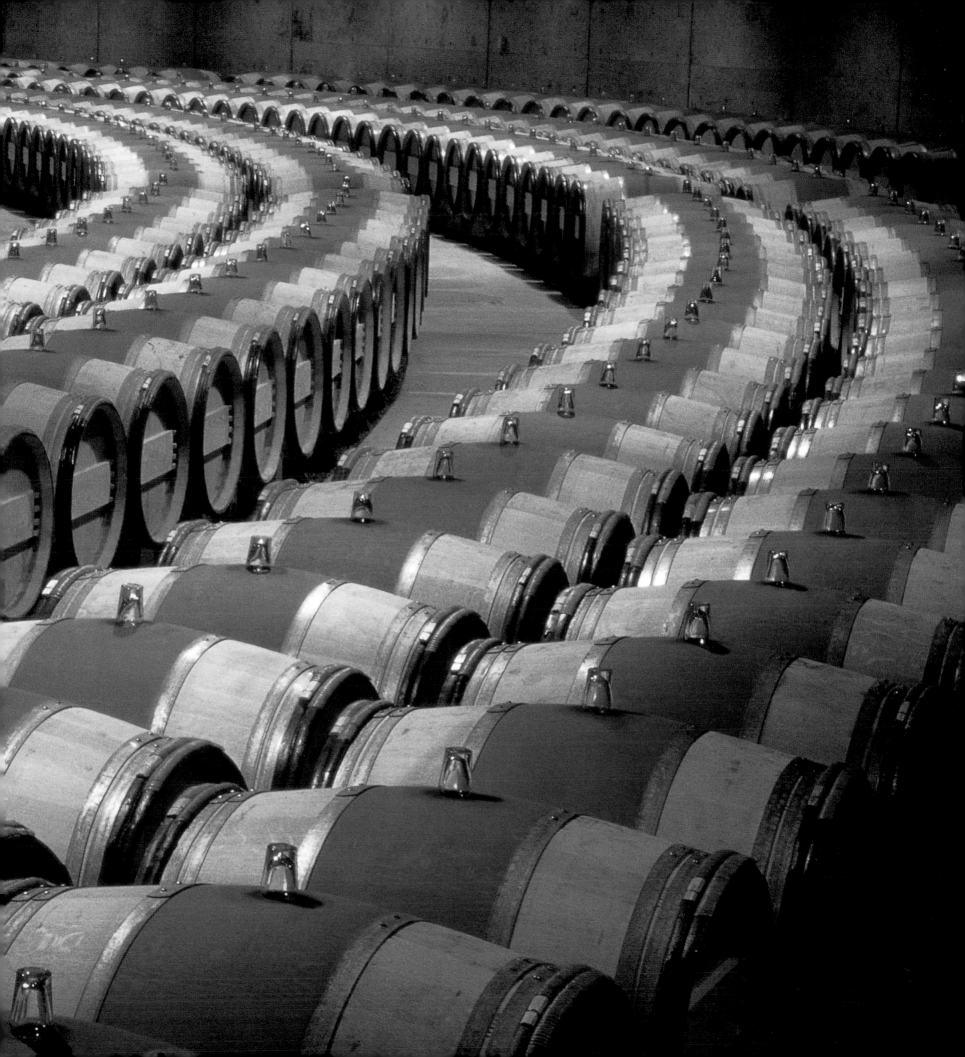

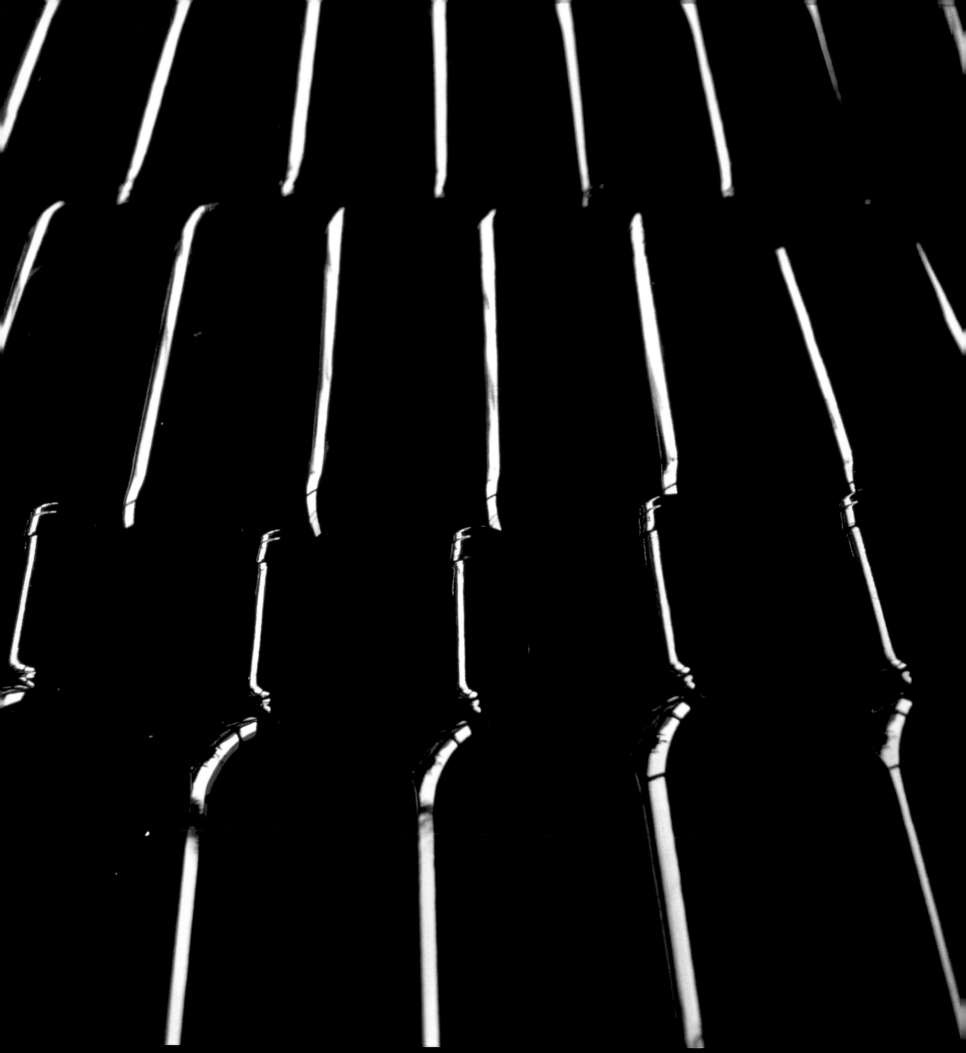

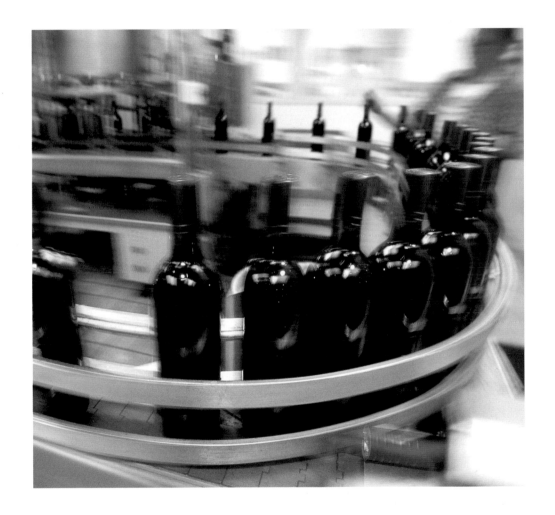

Filled bottles wait their turn for labels at a Spanish winery *(left)*. Producers often delay
the expense of preparing labels because the destination of the wine will determine the legal wording.
All governments have different rules for labeling imported wines. A high-speed bottling line
in St. Helena, California, fills as many as 100 bottles per minute *(above)*.

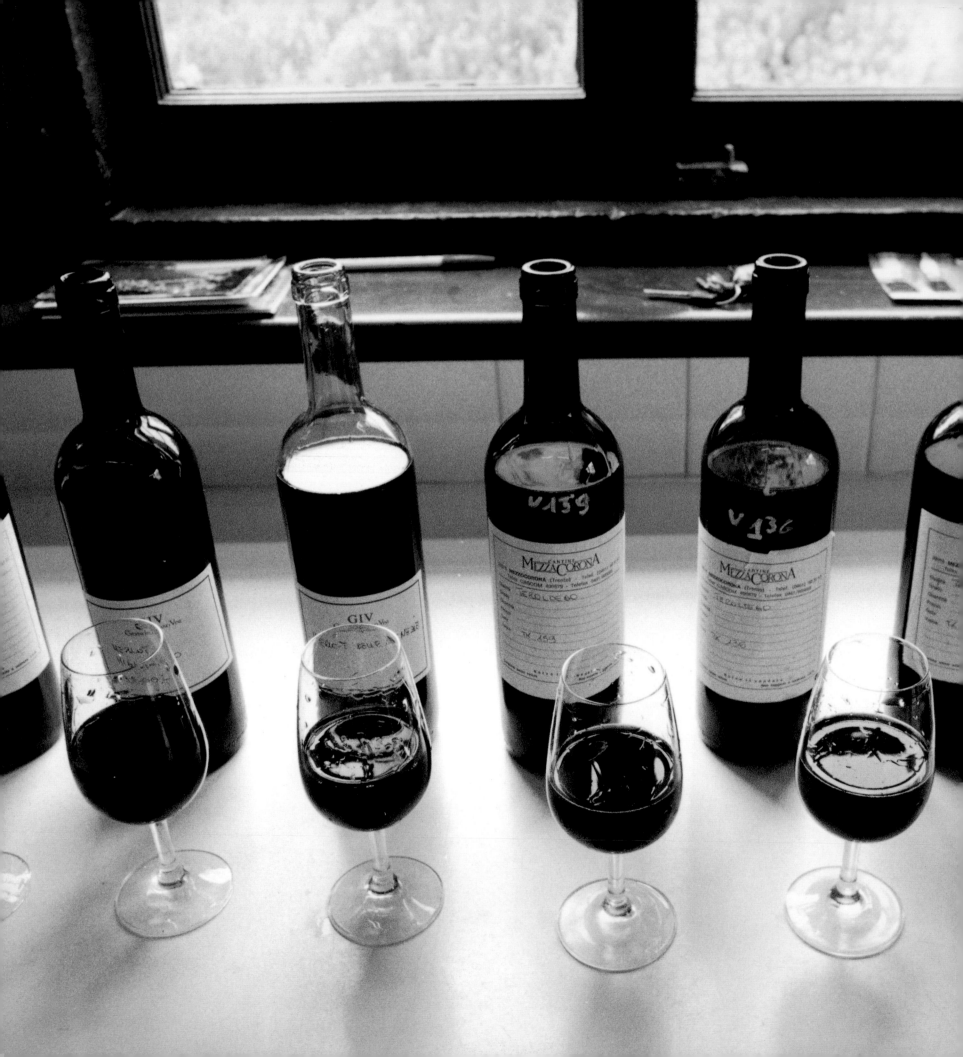

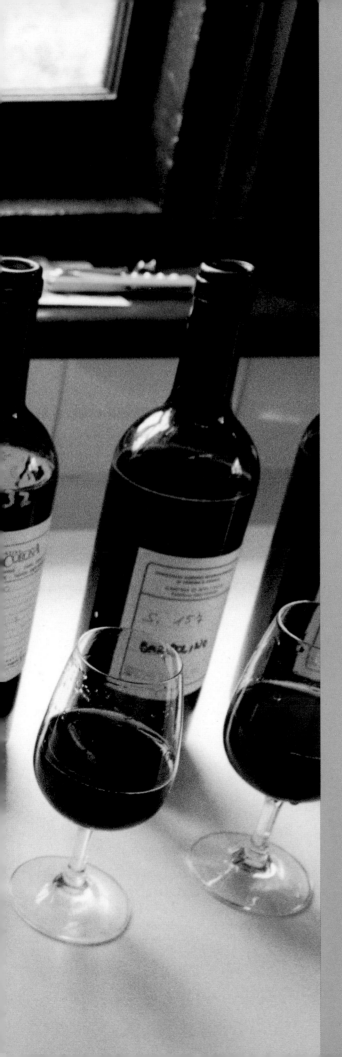

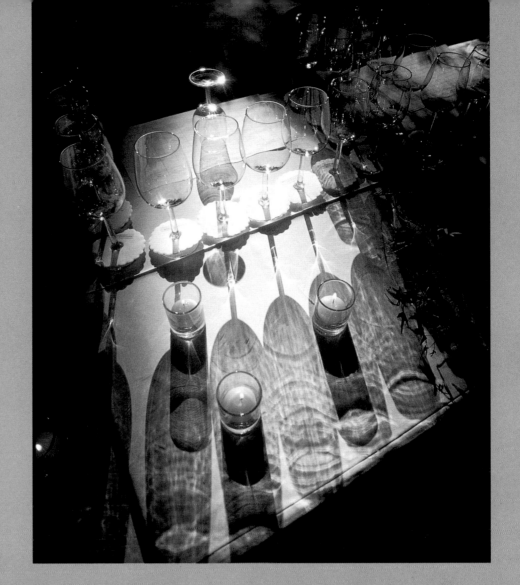

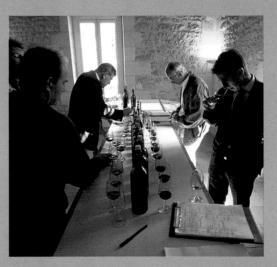

Blending, the last step that can determine a vintage's success, depends upon the judgment of master tasters. Wines from several vineyards await evaluation in the laboratory of Mount Hurtle Winery near Adelaide, Australia *(left)*. Owners and consultants taste samples around the blending bench at Cos d'Estournel, France *(above)*. The day's last rays of sun streak across glasses in a California winery *(top)*.

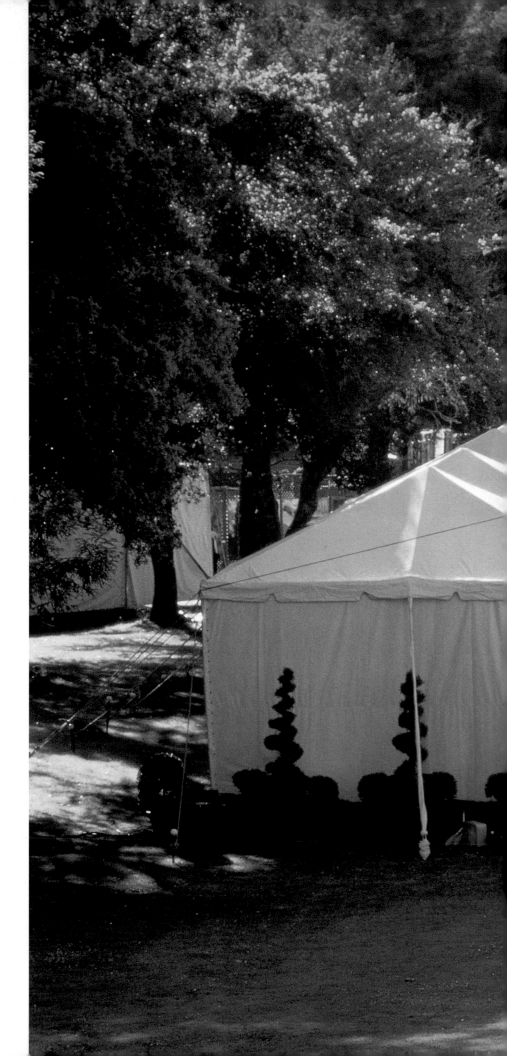

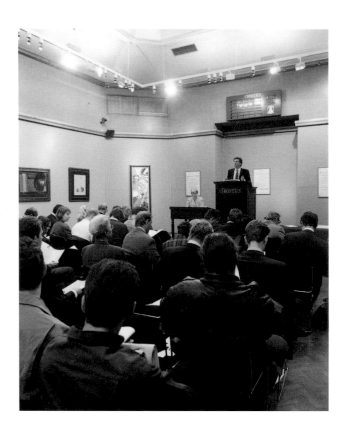

Part of the mystique of wine is the excitement and
expectation that surrounds the entire process. When it's time
to sell the product, auctions provide the platform to gauge
the true value of a great wine or to create enthusiasm
for vintages still seeking a market. The Christie's auction in
London brings out traditional buyers, as well as those
oenophiles with enough disposable income to pay thousands
of dollars for a bottle of outstanding Cabernet *(above)*.
The *al fresco* Napa Valley Wine Auction every June is part
social occasion, part business transaction, and
a great place to watch people *(right)*.

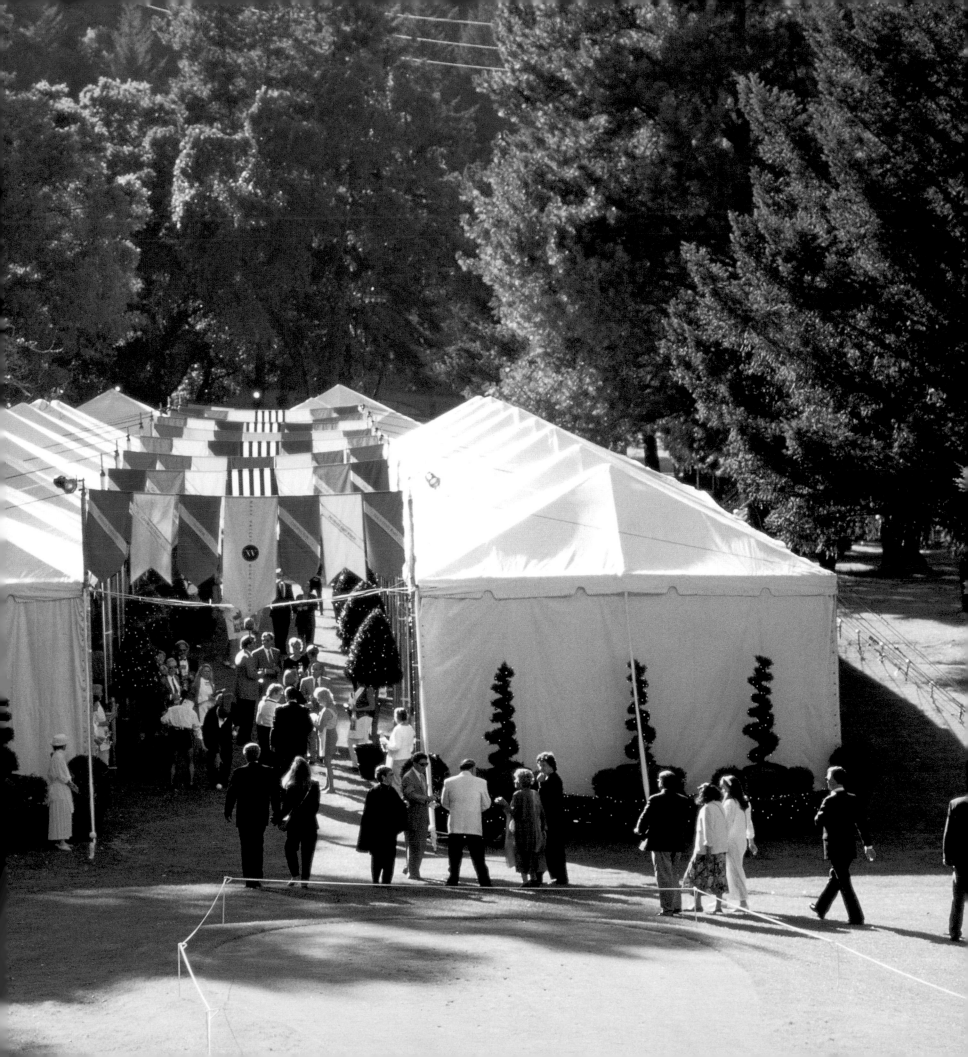

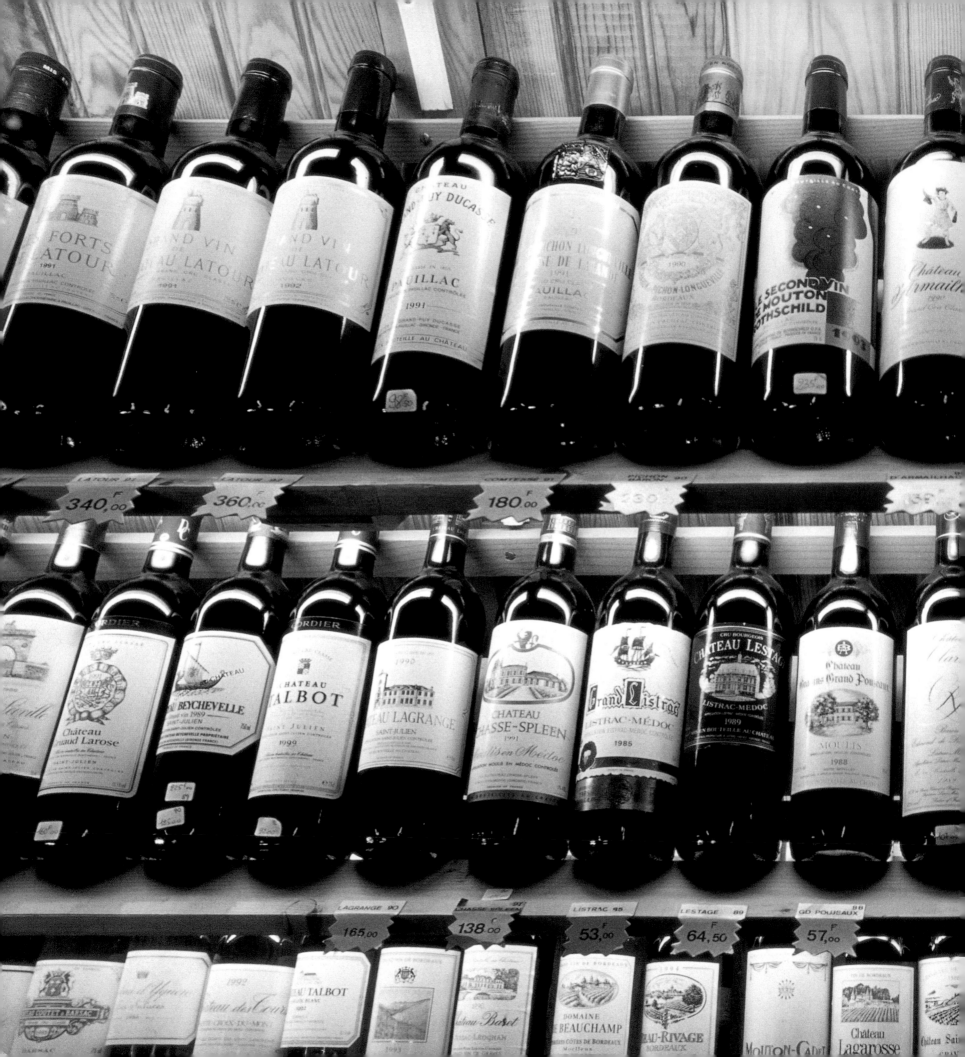

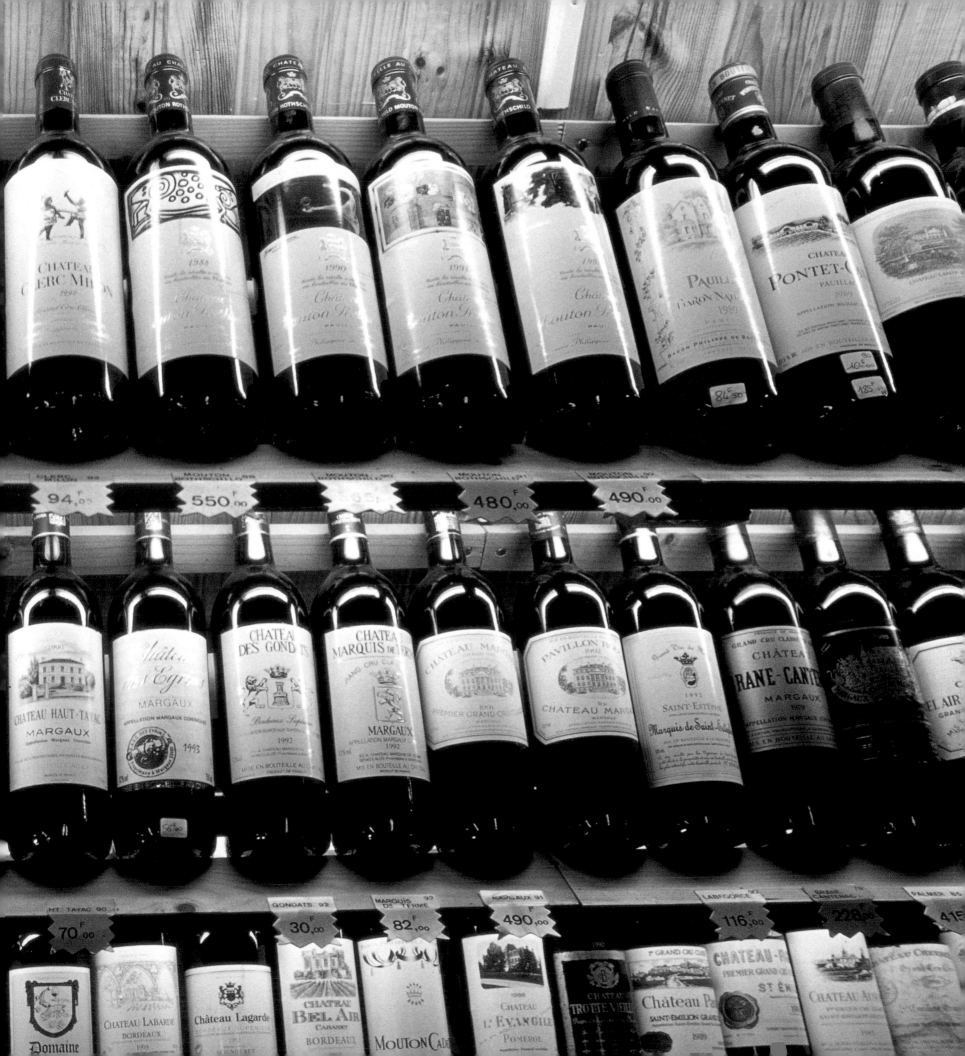

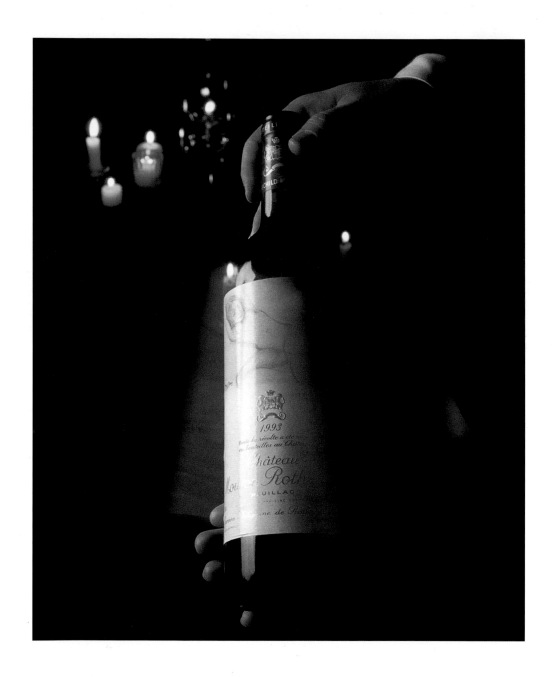

Is wine with a great history any better than wine with a great flavor? The cost of
a bottle of Cabernet does not necessarily coincide with its price in the market, and a famous
name on the label is not always a guarantee that the wine will be excellent. But in a selection
of famous Bordeaux blends at a wine specialty shop in Pauillac, the odds are good that
most of these bottles will contain outstanding Cabernet *(preceding pages)*. Presentation is part
of the performance. A Cabernet blend from Bordeaux is offered for approval at an upscale
dining room *(above)*. There are 15,000 bottles of wine representing 160 French vineyards in
the four-story display at L'Intendant in the city of Bordeaux *(right)*.

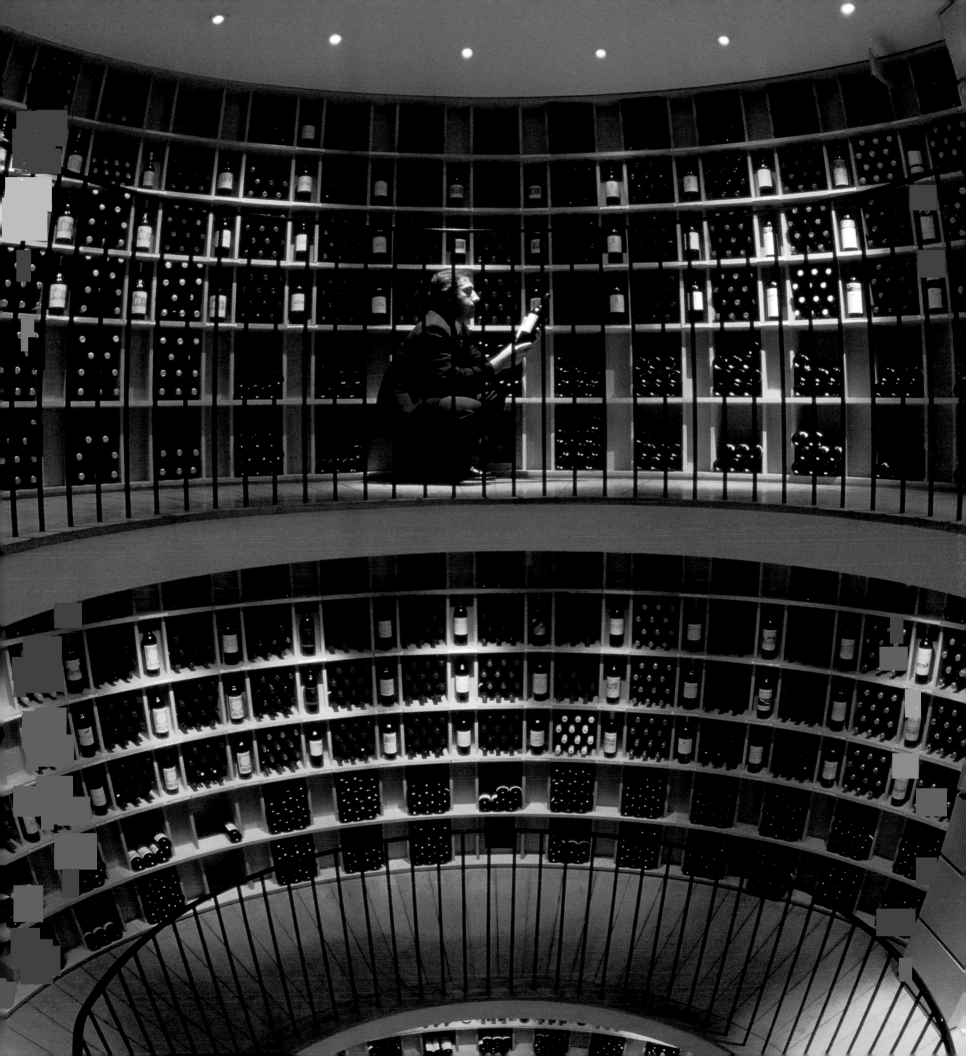

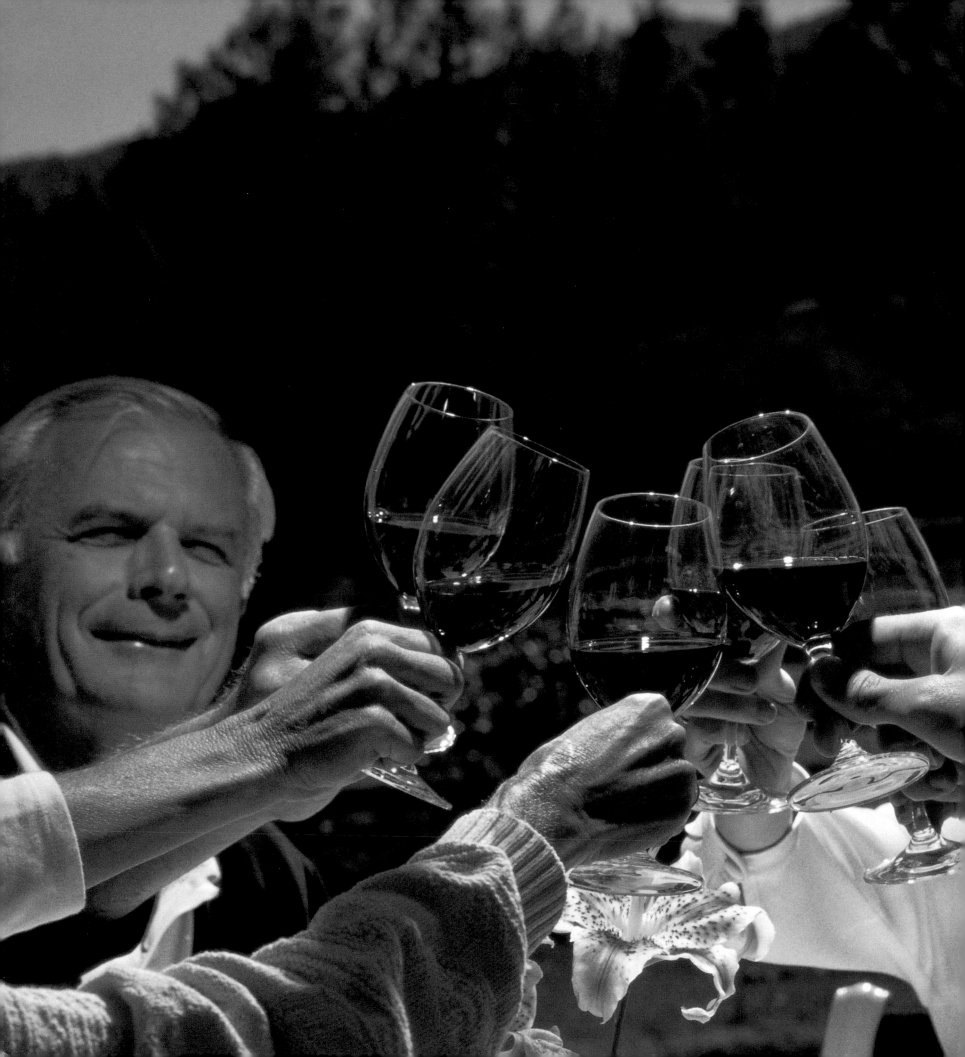

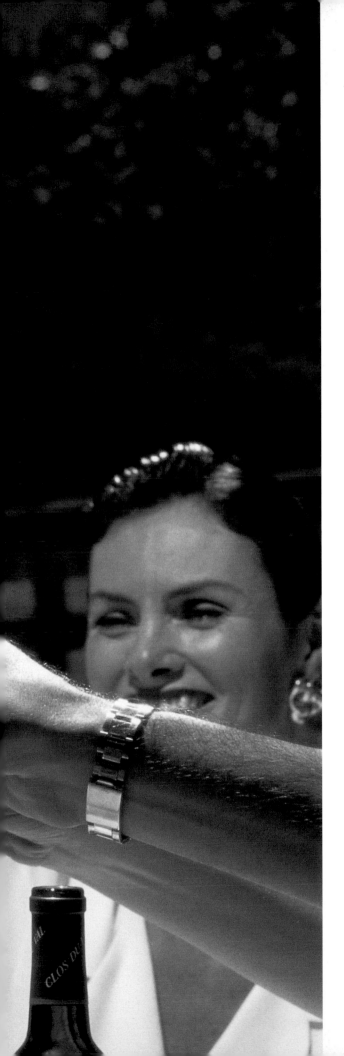

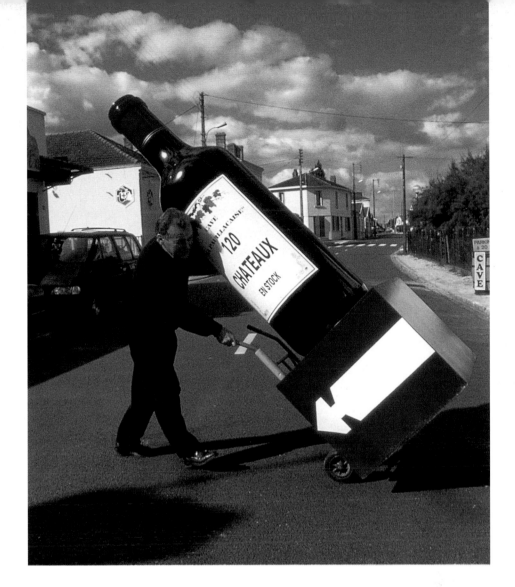

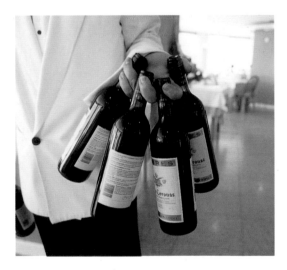

Happy faces, shining eyes, and gleaming glasses give purpose to the pursuit
of Cabernet's mystique *(left)*. The owner of the Cave la Pauillacaise in France rolls
out a giant replica of the traditional high-neck Bordeaux-style bottles that
are for sale inside his store *(top)*. It takes a deft hand for this Spanish waiter to
satisfy his customers' demands for more Cabernet *(above)*.

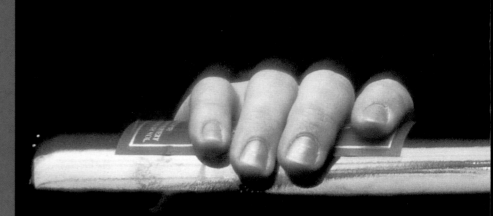

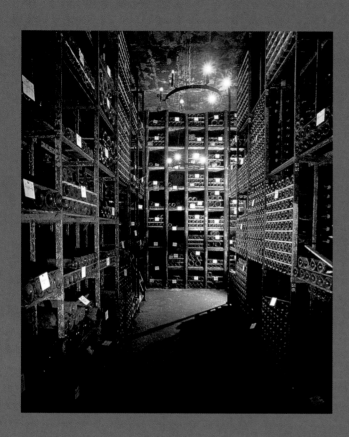

The bottle-aging cave at Château Mouton-Rothschild
in Bordeaux was sealed and hidden during World War II to
protect the vintages from invading Nazi troops. Today, it
serves as the highlight of a tour for VIP visitors *(above)*. Bottle
aging fine Cabernet usually creates sediment in the bottom
after several years. It is decanted in front of a light so only
clean wine is transferred *(right)*. At this point, the winemaking
process is almost complete. This vintage has had good fortune
throughout the process, from growing and harvesting the
grapes through fermenting and aging the wine. Now comes
the most important step of all—enjoying the wine.

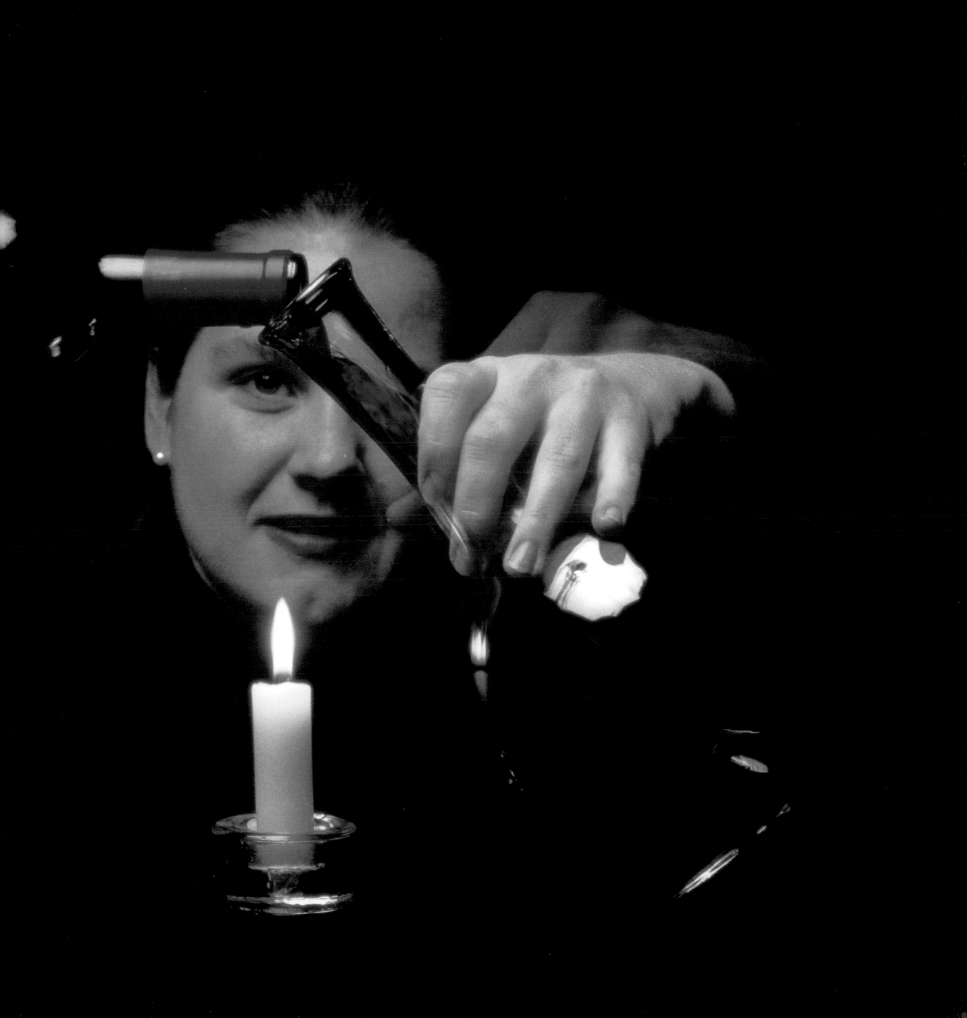

"A Cabernet Sauvignon is
at its best when allowed to
express time and place—
the circumstances of a
vintage, the characteristics
set by a vineyard."

GERALD ASHER
WINE EDITOR, *GOURMET* MAGAZINE

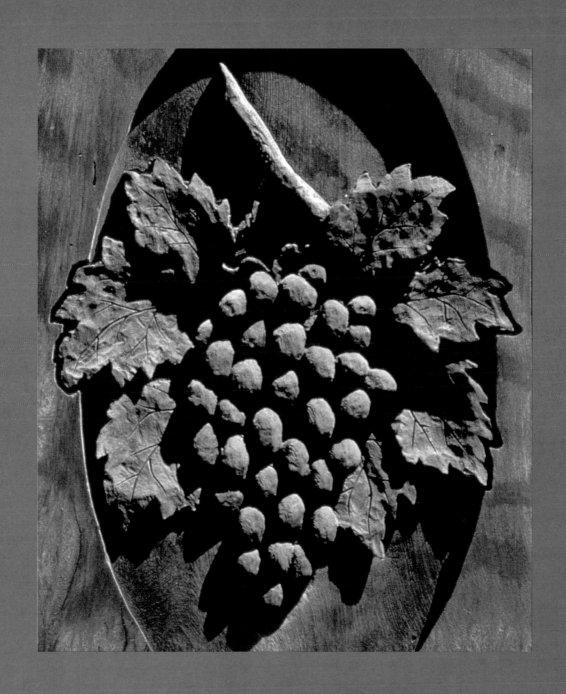

index

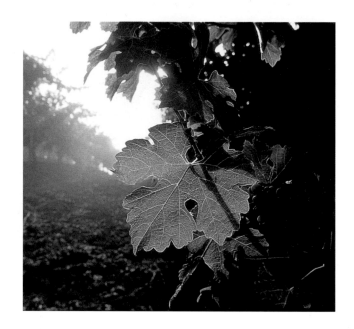

acknowledgments

I am extremely grateful to the many friends who shared my enthusiasm and my vision for this project. Worldwide photo coverage for many of these images was possible only with the support of the Corbis Corporation and especially the personal interest of Charles Mauzy. Taking photographs from most of the locations and wineries was made possible by generous and unselfish introductions from Bob and Margrit Mondavi. At *National Geographic* magazine, Bill Garrett and Bob Gilka first launched me into the study of wine when they assigned me to photograph Napa Valley in 1978. I want to thank Craig Aurness, Stephanie O'Rear, and Mike Carpenter in Los Angeles; Allen Boraiko in Santiago; Brett and Erica Newell, and Lisa VandeWater in New Zealand; Len Evans, and Peter and Margaret Lehmann in Australia; Win Scudder, Ellen Boughn, and Sid Hastings in Washington State; Lucie Morton in Virginia; Patrick and Marie-Christine Cronenberger, and Bruno Prats in France; Sue Greene, Peter Van Niekerk, and Clive Torr in South Africa; Jorge Grosse in Spain; and in Northern California Jerry Alexander, Mary Azevedo, Bill and Jane Ballentine, Jennifer Barry, Leslie Barry, Chris Burt, Michael Creedman, Chris Howell, Laura Hunt, Daphne Larkin, Chris Phelps, Valerie and Earle Presten, Tia O'Rear, Michael Raymor, Meg Smith, Jim Vestal, and Warren Winiarski.

Books I found valuable included *The Oxford Companion to Wine*, edited by Jancis Robinson, Oxford University Press, 1994; *A Practical Ampelography* by Pierre Galet, with translation by Lucie Morton, Cornell University, 1979; and *Cabernet Sauvignon* by Harry Eyres, Viking, 1991.

Additional photo credits:
Laura Hunt: Pages 72–73. Copyright Corbis: Pages 22, 33, 36, 39, 41, 60, 61 *(lower)*, 68, 76–77, 78 *(lower right)*, 81, 86 *(lower)*, 90 *(both)*, 92, 93, 94 *(lower)*, 101, 102 *(top)*, 106 *(top)*, 107, 109 *(top)*, 112–113, 118, 119 *(lower)*, 122 *(top)*, 123, 130, 137.